GOD IS REAL ...

"You don't even have to wonder"

Written By

CHONDREA BLACK

Inspired by

Corion D'Shawn Reed

A MEMOIR OF OUR JOURNEY

God is Real…You Don't Even Have to Wonder

ISBNs 979-8-9853320-0-1 (Paperback); 979-8-9853320-1-8 (eBook)

Editors & Consultants
Patricia St. Clair Eldridge, MBA
Seletha M. Head-Tucker, MS, M.Ed.,Owner/CEO, North Memphis
Publishing House

 Cover designed by All Occasion Printing & Design
www.aoprintdesign.com

Dedicated to...

This book is dedicated to my husband Robert, daughter Danielle, and grandchildren, Jacori, Jace, Aria, and the twins. Our fantastic support system included my sisters Crystal & Ericka, my in-laws affectionately called the Black Tribe, my close friends that never left my side, and the many nurses, CNAs, doctors, and dialysis staff who were kind, patient, and dedicated to Corion's care.

Our Journey...

Introduction...

On January 23, 2014, my son, Corion D'Shawn Reed, at twenty-six years old, was rushed to the hospital in sudden cardiac arrest and coded in the emergency room. The ER staff worked to resuscitate him for more than an hour. The doctor said he wouldn't shock him again, and I fell to my knees and prayed beside the gurney. He said, "I will shock him once more. Everyone move away from the bed." I turned to the wall to talk to the Lord. I said, "Lord, if it be your will, then I surrender to your will, but I truly believe that he can be a testimony to your kingdom." The doctor shocked him, and the machine started beeping. His heart was beating once again.

Corion lived for six (6) years after this incident, and over the years, he shared many things with me that I didn't understand. Despite kidney failure, global anoxic brain injury diagnosis, and gastro (stomach) issues, he thrived. The doctors suspected that the brain injury would cause him to be a vegetable and told us he would never be the same. But I had read an article in the waiting room about a man who was told his son would never be the same after sustaining a brain injury from a car accident. The father said to them, "He won't be the same. He'll be better." I believe God sent me that word to encourage me, as He sent me many more after that. Corion was far from a vegetable. He was not the same; he was better.

As a matter of fact, he said to me later that same year, *"MA! Write everything down. We gone change the world."* This book is a compilation of the many things Corion said to me, questions he asked, and how he and God brought me to a greater relationship with the Lord. My faith is greater, our family is stronger, my heart is better.

God has a purpose and a plan for all of us, no matter the situation or circumstance. He does not want us to live in fear and self-doubt. His word says, "For I know the plans I have for you; not to harm you; to give you hope and a future." I have learned that we can take Him at His word.

This memoir is my attempt to share my many special moments with Corion, framed by God's holy word. After Corion transitioned, I felt a strong anointing, and God began to pour out the interpretations of those moments into my spirit. I began to recognize how our journey had been framed by scripture.

I'd always known that this was bigger than us because God shared that with me early on, but the glory of it all must be shared as I've been instructed. I pray His glory is revealed through my obedience to His word.

This is our story.

11/16/2014 (social media post)

I am sincerely thankful to all of you who have allowed me to share my pics and this awesome day. Corion D'Shawn Reed is constantly trying to gain clarity and understanding of his "situation". Today he said to us with great sincerity that "God is REAL. He has everything laid out. You don't even have to wonder." I said boy don't make me shout he said gone and shout then. He told me and Robert that we "have a new person." I'll let the memory of this day carry me on thru. Please continue to pray for us as we pray for you.

Chapter 1

His Character, His Presence, His Language

"So we have come to know and to believe the love that God has for us. God is love, and whoever abides in love abides in God, and God abides in him." 1 John 4:16

Did you have the best grandmother ever? I sure did. She was an amazingly strong woman, and she taught us about God. When it came to her grandchildren, she made sure we ate well, were clean, had fun, got along with one another, and she always supported her children as best she could. She protected us and taught us to respect our elders. I know mine kept me from getting many spankings from my mom. And the food she cooked was always delicious. She had rules, and if you didn't follow them, you were disciplined, but not as often as you should have been. She was up when we got up and watched us fall asleep. And somehow, she still had time to see about others.

His Character

God's character is like that of a good grandmother. His word is his food, and it is so good. He has commandments that are our rules. His grace and mercy are our protection. And just like with our grandmothers, we don't understand what we have until it is taken away from us.

1

God is a loving Father that cares for your every need. He has left his word on record to lead and direct us through every area of our life. He will make the crooked paths straight.

He has done it for me, so I know He will do it for you, according to the measure of your faith. I believe He can do anything but fail. **To God be the GLORY!**

His Presence

I would visit Corion in the evenings to be sure he was fed well and was comfortable before going to sleep. It gave me comfort to know that he was well. We would laugh, joke, I could talk with him, and many times he was able to express to me how he was feeling. That would also spark many of my Facebook posts. It was our time together.

After he came home, there was one night I was sitting in his room as we were winding down for bed. We had the most amazing exchange. I thought he was falling asleep, so I was about to leave, and he said, "*Are you leaving?*" I replied, "Yes, do you need something?" And he thought for just a moment, sighed, and said, "*Just your presence, I guess.*" Wow!! What a beautiful expression of how he genuinely felt. Just my presence at that moment was enough for him. And his expression of that need and heartfelt love was enough for me to sit another hour.

I've since learned that the same love and comfort can be felt in God's presence. His presence is reassuring. Your connection to His character and voice becomes a sense of peace. You learn that it is not about the things of this world that show you who God is but knowing His presence despite the things. His word says that if we seek first the kingdom of God and his righteousness, all these "things" will be added unto us. Things are often referred to as material, but I believe He will also add the intangible things; love, joy, peace, understanding, longsuffering, endurance, and comfort of knowing Him. Getting in the presence of God is our protection from the evil of the day.

His Language

In learning God's voice, you can further get to understand his language. His language is his word. I remember early in the pandemic when God spoke to me and said to me, "Speak my language." I was still learning to acknowledge his voice. So, I began to ask questions.

How can I speak His language when I don't know His language? Then the spirit answered and said, "His language is His word." It was only a day or so later, while listening to a gospel radio program, I overheard the speaker say, "Lies are the language of the devil." So, I was able to surmise that God's word is the truth and His language, while the language of the enemy is lies. If it doesn't line up with the word of God, it is not Truth. We must develop a love for the TRUTH!!

The word tells us that God's people know his voice and another they will not follow. So, we must not only know God's voice but know his language through knowing His character. His character is much like that of a grandmother's love, His language is the word, the truth, and His voice is one of comfort, reassurance, and guidance. To make an assessment that you are hearing Him, understand the truth of his word, getting to know his character and hearing his voice, you must first get into his presence.

Seek Him

To get into the presence of God, there must be a genuine heart to seek after him. Many times, this genuine heart comes in a time of trouble. Times of trouble generally are when we don't have an answer nor know a way out. Here is when we drop the walls of fake and vain worship and forsake concern for what others may say or think.

We stop acting out the patterns, rituals, and ways of being that we learned when we "played church" as a child or even as an adult. There will come a time when playing is no longer acceptable, and you must get deeper and more serious to find relief from the pain and fear that is upon you in the moment.

In those times, we humble ourselves and shut out the world around us because we have a genuine need for truth and to be rescued. Therefore, so many "find" God in times of trouble. It's because NOW you are seeking his righteousness for that "thing" you need in the moment. You want to hear from that spiritual being you've learned about, no doubt from that loving and caring grandmother.

I was active in the church. If asked, my husband and children would even describe me as a "church lady". On occasion, I read the word. I prayed often but more as a "requirement", and not earnestly seeking Him. I would follow the rules and try to align my life and way of being with the acceptable doctrine of my denomination.

But at that moment in 2014, when my child's life, my son, my first born, was at stake, I went deeper. I didn't care about who was around me and what they thought, I didn't know exactly what to say or do, but I got down to business with God. I needed Him to do something for me. I needed to know if He was who I had come to know Him to be, and I wanted to see his cards.

Not only did I not want to lose my son, but I genuinely did not want his soul to reside in the hell my Pastor so often preached about. I believed His word to be true, so if I could "ask and receive", then I thought, what better time than this moment. Before, I had asked God for things like a house, cars, a better relationship with my spouse, to protect my kids. But this was life or death.

I am thankful for the Holy Spirit interceding for me, allowing God to see my heart, and answering my prayer. But in exchange, not only did He have a new thing for me, but also for Corion.

During his 2nd year of recovery, Corion told me one day when we were in the car, "*You was the only one who knew what to do*" at that moment. He said, "*No one else knew what to do, but you did. I love you for that.*" So that means he was well aware of what had happened. He may not have been able to articulate it, but he knew. He would tell me often, "*I know more than you think I know.*" He would also say, "*I know more than you.*" I believed that then, and I truly believe it now.

God took us this way for a reason, and things are still being revealed to me. But I wanted to at least write his story soon after his passing so that I would not forget the things that God has shown me. Also, none of us know the day or the hour, and I want to make haste to do God's will. I must do what it is God has for me to do. God has assured me that I am His child and that I have a job to do.

Chapter 2
The Shadow of Death

"Yea, though I walk through the valley of the shadow of death"
Psalms 23:4

I purchased a sign at Christmas time in 2013 that said, "Believe in Miracles". I loved the sign's colors and, to be honest, didn't think much about the words. I mean, I would say out of my mouth that I believed in miracles. Still, I hadn't ever really experienced anything that I would call a miracle. I had heard others talk about miracles at church. In fact, the name of my church is Miracle Temple Church of God in Christ. There were many testimonies of "miracles," but they were all secondhand for me, but I did believe the people.

The following year, my family experienced a miracle firsthand. We would definitely add to the many miraculous testimonies spoken of at our church. I can now say without any doubt that this sign is true. I can say unequivocally that I believe in miracles. To God be the GLORY!

There will come a time in this life when you must trust God's will and not your own. There are limitations in our human frailty as men and women, and even with our best intentions, we cannot see nor do what God can. My family found this to be oh so true as we were so unexpectedly confronted with a life-or-death moment. Only a few close family and friends have come from behind the veil of the computer screen of Facebook to know the details of our story. Many have followed along on social media pondering how we maintained faith and hope in the most devastating and unfair tragedy. To get to the good days was a real battle. Still, we held to our belief that God is doing a great work, and we longed to see something extraordinary come from what admittedly felt catastrophic.

On January 23, 2014, my son Corion experienced a sudden cardiac arrest in the hospital's emergency room he had been recently discharged from two days earlier. You see, he had a pericardial window procedure to drain fluid from around his heart. He understood that this procedure was an emergency and would prevent him from having an impending heart attack. In recovery, after the procedure, I was told by the doctor that he had "a 1 in 1000% chance of having a heart attack". Well, I guess he was THE ONE. But God!

Corion chose this hospital because his grandmother, Jackie, had surgery there that week. He didn't want to inconvenience the family in having to be in two separate places. He was always considerate in that way.

Jackie's procedure was a mastectomy that became more complicated than expected. She was in excruciating pain after the procedure. Corion was receiving updates as he lay in the bed in a different hospital wing. Once he heard that she wasn't well, he strongly insisted on seeing her, but there was a problem. He was not allowed to walk around, as he still had a tube in his chest draining the fluid from around his heart. But the response, "there is nothing we can do," was hardly an acceptable answer for him when it came to his loved ones, especially concerning *"Grannyma,"* as he affectionately called her.

In response to his persistence, the nurse finally obliged his request by wheeling him over in his bed to the Women's Wing in a completely different building on the other side of the hospital. The moment was priceless, and me being his mother with a love of photos, I snapped a picture to record this moment in time. Still in his hospital gown and socks, he most certainly wasn't pleased with my taking a photo, but little did we know at the time, this would be the last photo of them captured in the same frame.

Over the next few days, Jackie, my mom, would undergo a second surgery which landed her in the ICU with pulmonary edema. She had to spend about a week on a ventilator. This was our first experience with a loved one on a ventilator and sick at this level, unfortunately, it would not be our last. She soon recovered and was moved to the noncritical patient unit. Meanwhile, Corion had been discharged from the hospital on Tuesday and was able to drive himself home.

He went to dialysis the next day for his scheduled treatment. Afterward, he came to visit mom at the hospital. He expressed that he did not feel well and walked slower than normal. Observing his distress, his Aunt Ericka drove him home. I wish I had insisted that he see the doctor, but it didn't even cross my mind at the time. I was still worried about how Corion looked earlier, when I was startled by his late-night phone call. But he assured me he was "fine." He must have sensed my distress because he said that he was just checking on me, and wanted to tell me that he loved me. My sweet boy always loved his mother, even though he would just as consistently give me the blues. As I think back now, that was the last phone call I received from him on his own accord. Little did we know we were standing in the shadow of death.

Chapter 3
He Shall Live and Not Die

"I shall not die, but live, and declare the works of the Lord."
Psalm 118:17

The next day, a Thursday, Corion was home with my sister, Ericka. She noticed that he was sweating quite a bit and asked him if he was all right. He complained of chest pains and really didn't appear to be well at all, so she promptly called an ambulance. The ambulance arrived within minutes. He could walk, so the paramedics escorted him inside the ambulance, however, she became even more concerned because they sat there, in front of the house for a long time. What were they doing? Was he ok? She began to worry even more. They finally turned on the sirens and headed to the emergency room as she followed close behind.

After being rushed into the ER, the EMTs wheeled him into a small room. There was a lot of construction taking place both inside and outside of the building. An ER nurse began asking him the routine questions to determine the problem, but amid the triage, he grabbed his chest and fell back on the bed. The attending staff called for help, and the room began to swell with nurses, paramedics, and the physician.

The emergency staff immediately began resuscitation procedures. There were many medical terms spoken, but Ericka understood that he had stopped breathing. They began chest compressions, and she heard their

9

request that he be intubated. This young man of 26 years old, her only nephew, her sister's oldest child and only son, was experiencing a sudden cardiac arrest. Even after having a procedure, he was assured would prevent this very incident, his heart stopped beating. She could not believe this was happening.

Meanwhile, I was at work that day feeling certain that my mom and Corion were both on the road to recovery. So much so, during my lunch break, I went to Walgreens to pick up some cards because Valentine's Day was approaching. When I returned from lunch, I received a call from my sister, Ericka. I could quickly tell that she was upset.

In my mind, I assumed she was updating me on our mother, but with so much grace, she quickly said, "I need you to listen to me. We are at Methodist Germantown. Corion's heart stopped in the emergency room." I hung up and screamed, "Lord, I can't take anymore!" I was in disbelief, but I called my husband, Robert, and told him the same thing just as quickly and with as much grace as I could muster at that moment, and I hung up.

I needed to get to Corion. I wanted to scream, run, and cry out loud to release the emotions that had quickly consumed my mind. But there was no time for that. I yelled for someone in my office to drive me to the ER, which was about 10 minutes away. In this moment of panic, I knew that I could not do this alone. This would be the longest 10 minutes of my life.

I didn't want to allow my mind to even ponder the thought of him not breathing or his heart not beating. I refused to succumb to the feeling that this was the end for my son. We were about halfway there when my co-worker, Stacy, a true prayer warrior, began to pray aloud. She said a lot of words. I couldn't focus on much, but I clung to her saying, "He shall live and not die". I buried it deep inside my heart and repeated it to myself over and over, and for many days to follow.

When I entered the ER, my sister met me at the door accompanied by the chaplain awaiting my arrival. They took me to the room where my son's limp body lay with a medical professional on top of him, desperately performing chest compressions as if he had a personal stake in the life of this young man. I can still see the intensity in his face as he worked to get him back.

As I walked into the room, I yelled out to my boy, "Corion, GET UP! Corion, get up NOW," as if he were late for school and about to miss the bus or lying there pulling a prank on everyone. Like he would just arise at my command. What did I expect? Did I expect that he would hear the very familiar voice of his mother and get up? I don't know what I was thinking, but I knew I needed to pray. And I did.

I fell to my knees and began to pray, but they lifted me from the floor, demanding that I could not stay there. What do you mean, I can't stay here...in the middle of the floor, praying to God? Here, on the floor of the ER where my son's lifeless body was lying on a gurney, with nurses and paramedics and a doctor standing in the corner almost as if he were skillfully directing traffic?

But I had to pray. I didn't know anything else to do. But what I did know was that God was the only one that could help me, us, and him in this moment. I pleaded for a place where I could pray. They took me and my sister into another room. She and I kneeled on the floor beside the bed and continued to pray.

As I prayed, I could still hear the concerned voices as they ushered Robert into the room. I could feel him standing beside me, and with my eyes barely open, I grabbed his hand, pulling him to the floor to join me. I then heard a voice which I assume was a nurse tell us that they got a pulse. I praised God, but I did not stop praying. I was looking for more confirmation. It didn't feel complete.

Within what felt like seconds they came back and said they lost him again. I continued to pray and plead with God that he change his mind about Corion's fate. They urged us to come into the room where we had just witnessed the saddest sight we could have imagined at that moment. I didn't want to go back in; I didn't want to see him in this state of lifelessness anymore.

Chapter 4

A Testimony to His Kingdom

"Thy kingdom come, thy will be done in earth, as it is in heaven." Matthew 6:10

When I think back, I remember feeling so helpless. The feeling of helplessness is a very familiar feeling for me. It's a feeling I felt from childhood, and I swore that I would never revisit as an adult. Lord, what is happening here, was my cry. Haven't I experienced enough hurt in my life already? In my mind, I thought, this is not how my life is supposed to be as I serve a mighty God. He has always answered my prayers. There must be something else I can do.

Convinced that I had no other option, I followed the nurse, chaplain, my sister, and husband as we were led back into the room where Corion lay. Through tearful eyes and my own mumbled prayers, I heard the doctor declare that he was not going to shock him again. As evidenced by the bruises on his chest, he had done it a few times already.

Unsure of what to do next, I remembered a conversation with my sister-in-law, Lisa, when she shared with me, "If you pray in the spirit, the devil can't hear your prayer." I then kneeled beside the gurney where my son lay still lifeless, and I began to pray in the spirit. As I understood it at the time, praying in the spirit was speaking to God in a language in which only the Holy Spirit could understand and interpret on my behalf. I recently learned of a great description of it in Romans.

Romans 8:26-27
"We do not know what we ought to pray for, but the Spirit himself intercedes for us through wordless groans. And he who searches our hearts knows the mind of the Spirit, because the Spirit intercedes for God's people in accordance with the will of God."

Surrendered to His Will

After what felt like only a few moments of prayer, I imagine the doctor's heart was pricked, and going against his earlier declaration, decided to shock him once more. "Everyone step back", he commanded. I then stood up, stepped back, turned to the wall, made a last plea to the Lord, and said, "Lord, if this be your will (death), I surrender to your will, but I truly believe that he can be a testimony to your kingdom."

The doctor shocked him, and the machine began to beep, signifying that there was a heartbeat. At that moment, it was as if time stood still, and everyone was frozen. The doctor then said that we could have some time with him. I went over to him and held his cold hand and kissed his face. I told him if he could hear me, then talk to the Lord, repent of his sins, and ask God to come into his heart. I didn't get a response.

Robert, my sister, and I just sat there with him, not knowing if he would be ok or even if his heart would continue to beat. Our Pastor, Elder Sylvester Hamilton, made it there and prayed with us. I never found out how he knew what was happening. He was like a grandfather to Corion, and I called him "Father". He was always there when we needed him and imparted great spiritual wisdom and love to our family.

Shortly after the Pastor left, the surgeon who had performed his pericardial procedure came in to check him and asked us to leave the room. We sat outside his room in hard chairs near an entrance covered with large clear construction plastic. During this time, the nurses, out of concern, asked if they could do anything for us? My only request was that they pray, as everything was in God's hands. One nurse shared with us that she had never witnessed anyone pray like that before. As she showed me the goosebumps on her arm, she stated, "You truly have a connection with your son and with the Lord. We got a pulse back the first time you entered the room and called his name."

We later learned that they worked on him for more than an hour. More time than they would normally spend doing resuscitation. I am told they generally don't go past about 30 to 45 minutes. But they were persistent because of his age.

I am thankful that they did not give up. At that time, my sister, Crystal said, "If these strangers wouldn't give up on him, then how can we." I continued to pray to the Lord saying, "Lord, I trust you. He shall live and not die." AMEN

2020 Hindsight

After this miraculous moment and the many moments afterward, I was constantly assured that we were in the midst of a miracle. We all experienced it in that room in the ER that day; all of us together. God restored life where there was none through persistence, fervent prayer, and agreement. We were all in agreement that this young man should live. The staff was persistent with life-saving measures, and my family was in fervent prayer.

God's presence was with me when I entered the room. I now understand that my friend, Stacy, who drove me to the hospital, had invited Him into our situation when she began to pray. The Holy Spirit within allowed me to speak with all sincerity and power that day to command him to get up.

In May of 2020, while at home during the pandemic, Corion reminded me of not only what I said, but *how* I said it. The fact that he remembered is a miracle in itself. But he said to me, *"Mama, you said Corion, Get Up! Corion, Get up Now! That's why I came back."*

It wasn't until after Corion's transition and listening to a sermon that I realized Peter used these very same words in the book of Acts chapter nine. A certain disciple named Tabitha, which by interpretation is called Dorcas, was full of good works and alms deeds which she did. And it came to pass in those days that she was sick and died. In the message I was listening to, at the time, the Pastor read from the bible, which said, **He turned to the body and said, "Tabitha, get up."** I was floored. I had no idea at the time that this passage read this way!

I recently read in Mark 5, when Jesus arrived at Jarius' house, the people gathered were mourning and were preparing for his young daughter's funeral. The crowd laughed when Jesus exclaimed that the child was only sleeping and was not dead. He then took his closest disciples - Peter, James and John (the inner circle) - and the child's parents into the room. He took the child by the hand and said to her, "Talitha, cumi!" (which means "Little girl, get up!").

Also, during this time, the Holy Spirit revealed to me how Hezekiah, in 2 Kings 20:2-3, turned his face to the wall as he pleaded with God for more time. I too turned to the wall when I pleaded for Corion's life in the ER after his heart had stopped. God answered Hezekiah's prayer and granted him more time as he bitterly wept. I too benefited from this promise for my son. But I did not know about this scripture until now.

2 Kings 20:2-6
Hezekiah turned his face to the wall and prayed to
the Lord, "Remember, Lord, how I have walked before you faithfully and
with wholehearted devotion and have done what is good in your eyes." And
Hezekiah wept bitterly. Before Isaiah had left the middle courtyard, the
word of the LORD came to him, saying, "Go back and tell Hezekiah the
leader of My people that this is what the LORD, the God of your father
David, says: 'I have heard your prayer; I have seen your tears. I will surely
heal you. On the third day from now you will go up to the house of the
LORD. I will add fifteen years to your life. And I will deliver you and this city
from the hand of the king of Assyria. I will defend this city for My sake and
for the sake of My servant David.'"

Do you remember when you were in trouble, and God came for you? You don't have to deserve it or do everything right for God to work in your favor. God's word is full of love and compassion for His people. We must trust, believe, and take Him at his word.

Chapter 5

His Messengers

"Do not forget to show hospitality to strangers, for by doing so some people have shown hospitality to angels without knowing it." Heb 13:2

After about an hour or so in the ER, his heart was still beating, so they began to transfer Corion to ICU. In the elevator during the transport, I was comforting Corion, letting him know that we were with him when I said his name. There was a paramedic that looked about Corion's age standing at the head of the transport bed. I could tell by the look on this young man's face that he knew that name.

Wide-eyed, he asked, "What's his name?" I responded, "Corion. You know him, don't you?" I could see the emotion in his expression change as this was no longer just another patient he was transporting; this was someone he knew personally. He said, "Yes ma'am. We play basketball together at World Overcomers sometimes." We had lived in the same neighborhood of Southeast Memphis since Corion was in grade school. He was always well known. As it's often said, he never met a stranger.

Robert, Ericka, and I were instructed to wait in an ICU family room nearby as they prepared Corion for inpatient care. After completing the transfer, the friend came into the family room and asked to speak with us. He said, "I heard he has a praying mother. I have a praying mother too."

He went on to say he had experienced several health-related, near-death experiences. He encouraged us to keep praying and believe things would be all right. He knew Corion to be a strong young man much like himself. This was the first of many encouraging experiences with strangers that helped to walk us through this season.

Later that evening, in the waiting room, the hospital security guard shared a story with Ericka of his son's near-death experience. Apparently, his son had suffered a similar fate as Corion, but he comforted her confirming his son had recovered and was doing well. He was yet another messenger from the Lord that all things will be well.

As the evening wore on, Ericka and I found the hospital chapel where we could pray and thank God for His glory on that day. While praying, I could sense the presence of another person entering the chapel. As I had begun to pray aloud, I could hear her join in and stand in agreement as if she knew my plight. At some point, we embraced, and I soon realized it was one of my closest friends, Michele. I told her earlier on the phone that she didn't have to come, but I am so grateful to God that she didn't listen to me.

God knows our needs, and He will send the right people at the right time to help hold you up when you least expect it. We always think that things happen by chance, but nothing is by chance. God is strategic, and He knows the plans He has for our lives. He places everyone in the right places at the right time so that His will is done.

This journey has taught me how much we are all connected. Corion confirmed that to me during one of our later stints in the hospital, but I'll get into that later. Strangers continue to encourage us to this day.

These encounters have increased my compassion for others, particularly those having trouble and experiencing the moments of uncertainty this life brings. It's normal in times like these to not know what to do or what you need, and the last thing you want to hear is "call me if you need something." No one knows what they need at a time like this, and much less would even think of calling someone.

I did not know what I needed in those moments. God made provisions through the many He sent to see about us in that time. They provided so much encouragement and strength and fueled our faith. I fondly recall the many hours Robert's cousin, Melissa, would come by the hospital, bring us food, and just keep us company in the waiting room. We had only recently connected with that side of his family. But God knows our needs before we do. You never know why someone comes into your life when they do. I've learned to cherish every relationship after that. We all need help at some point.

From now on, when I see a need, I just do what I can do at that moment, whether it is financial, a visit, a phone call or just a text. If nothing else, the word tells us that we ought always to pray (Luke 18:1). From my experience, the people that did things without us asking, sitting in the waiting room with us for many days, bringing us food, visiting, and especially those that simply prayed with us, are the people I remember and cherish most.

01/28/2014 (social media post)
Just got a visit from one of the ER nurses that was there when Corion
Reed came in. She says that they are still in awe of the miracle they
witnessed on Jan 23rd. She said that his still being here is NOTHING
they did; it is ALL GOD! Oh, how my faith is strengthened once
again!

Squeeze My Hand, Corion

They were ready for us to come into his room soon after the visit with his friend, the paramedic. I tried not to absorb the space's starch, empty, harsh coldness as we entered the room. I noticed that he was only connected to the breathing machine. No IV, no bags of fluid, no heart monitors like my mom had. I said to Robert, "They don't expect him to make it through the night."

We called Danielle, his sister, to meet us at the hospital. She was about six months pregnant with her first child. I didn't tell her why, I just told her to come after she got off work. Once she arrived, I explained what had happened. I didn't want to tell her on the phone because I knew it would be too much for her to bear alone. I needed to hold her and comfort her. She loved her big brother so much.

We all slept in the ICU room with Corion that night. Dani laid on a hospital couch while I opted for the chair. I remember Robert standing near the bed talking to his son as he laid there motionless.

We had decided many years ago not to use the term "step-father" in our home. When Corion was growing up, he worked hard to find the name that felt right for him. Sometimes he would call Robert by name, and other times he would refer to him as Daddy. As a teenager, he settled on "Pop."

As he leaned over the bed, Pop assured his son that he was there with him and wasn't going to leave his side. He made a pallet of blankets on the cold hard floor and slept next to his hospital bed. As long as we were all together, nothing else mattered.

1/25/14 (social media post)
Love is.......A father that makes a pallet on the hospital floor at his son's bedside because he promised not to leave him.

Before dawn the next morning, the lights flicked on, and in walked the neurologist and his team. He briefly greeted us and then began to assess Corion. "What is his name?" he asked. "Corion," I replied. In his strong foreign accent, he said, "Squeeze my hand Corion. Corion! Squeeze my hand." There was no response. Then he advised us that he would give him 48-72 hours to recover before he returns. He was sure to let us know that he wasn't confident that he would ever wake up.

Are you serious? First of all, we weren't the patient and had to gather ourselves before we could respond to his question, and we hadn't suffered the trauma Corion had experienced. How did he expect the patient to respond in that 60-second evaluation? They had already explained to us that he may have suffered hypoxic/anoxic global brain damage.

Anoxic Brain Injury occurs when the brain receives inadequate oxygen levels, usually following cardiac arrest when there is minimal to no blood reaching the brain. This was the case for Corion. Since then, I've learned that anoxic brain injury is not given the same attention as traumatic brain injury (TBI). It is an uphill battle getting the necessary care, assistance, and therapy needed in the case of anoxic brain injury patients.

I was fortunate enough to find an amazing Facebook group of Anoxic Brain Injury Caregivers. They were like group therapy for me. They also became a great source of information and support. I often called them my village. They were able to understand many of the struggles we all faced during this time.

Regardless of the diagnosis or prognosis, he was eventually able to squeeze my hand. That's all the strength I needed to know he was still with us and that we were pushing forward in faith and hope in God.

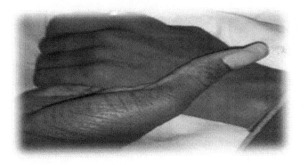

Chapter 6
His Plans

"For as the heavens are higher than the earth, so are my ways higher than your ways, and my thoughts than your thoughts."
Isaiah 55:9

God hears our prayers, He searches our hearts, He looks past our issues, and He loves us unconditionally. Most importantly, He knows the plans He has for us, not to harm us but to give us hope and a future. I learned that scripture during our time in the hospital and taped it to the wall in Corion's room in the intensive care unit (ICU).

I wanted everyone who entered the room to know that God's presence was there. It was also a constant reminder that a miracle had taken place. To the staff, this may have been an ordinary moment in the ICU, but for us, it was an extraordinary moment in our lives.

Our family began to gather at the hospital. We filled the ICU waiting rooms for days. Corion's biological father, Leland (Cory), was called from Atlanta as we were unsure what would happen. I've been told, when he came into the room, Corion briefly opened his eyes. He stayed with him in the hospital for several months, caring for him. He was also Corion's kidney donor in 2011. He turned out to be a great caregiver for Corion over the days, weeks and months to come. God will provide.

When you know God has done something incredible in your life, hold strong to your faith. I can recall the day one extremely condescending floor nurse doubtfully asked me, "Do you understand what is happening? Do you know that he may not be ok?" With a genuine smile, I assured her that I did understand completely and that my faith assured me God was in control. As she walked away from me with a distinct eye-roll, I whispered a prayer to my Father, "Do it for HER Lord. You are doing it for her."

It's Not for Us

As believers, we must remember that our lives and victories are not for us but for others. I asked God, "Why Lord? Why did you choose to bring Corion back?" Here we are, listening to grim diagnoses from the doctors and nurses. We are constantly being urged to take him off the ventilator. We are told that he may be brain dead and may remain in a vegetative state. Why??

We can ask questions of God without questioning Him. I know I've been taught not to question God, but I needed some assurance to what I know He clearly did in the ER just days earlier. I know it was an answer to my prayer, and in my heart, He knew that I was not being ungrateful. After several days, I just couldn't understand why He would still be on the breathing machine and not responding to commands from the doctors.

And just as a loving Father would, God answered my question. The Spirit said, "It's bigger than you and him. It is so that the young people will know that I (God) am REAL; as there are many that do not believe."

That was the first time I posted about our journey on Facebook. It was for the young people. That was my confirmation that this journey was extraordinary and that it was not just about us but an assignment from the Lord.

I was reminded of this in later years by my sister-in-law, LaKitta (aka Keke). She said to me, "Corion is not here for himself. He is here for us." She didn't know what God had shared with me years before. Then again, in November 2018, after Thanksgiving, during one of our numerous stints in the hospital, Corion confirmed to me himself.

People could never understand the joy I had, as they only saw and imagined what we were going through from their viewpoint. But having the joy of the Lord as my strength, and knowing that, even though this was so very difficult, and at times seemed too much to bear, I had the assurance through faith, countless confirmations and especially from my son's own words, that God was in control, and that we didn't have to worry. Corion said, *"God has everything under control. Don't worry about nothing."* "Nothing?" I asked. He replied, *"Not a thing."*

Youth Attack

God is pouring out His Spirit in this season, as we are in spiritual warfare. We must use the spiritual weapons He provides to fight spiritual battles. Many spirits are attacking our youth that they don't realize are coming against them, and even as mature believers, many times neither do we. The Holy Spirit said to me that God will not hold them accountable for the things coming against them that they can't fight.

As our teens become adults, I believe we should have more honest, open, and vulnerable conversations with them about our lives. We should be apologetic, when necessary, about some of our negative behaviors and projections that we now understand could have been handled differently. Don't act as if we had things all figured out when we were their age because we didn't. They may not be as respectful as we were at their age. But we must remember that the attack on their lives may be stronger than the spiritual battles we had to fight. The enemy's time to rule is coming to a close, and the spiritual fight is much stronger than generations before this time.

I can remember feeling like my mom didn't understand me and wanted her way, rather than allow what was pulling me another way. Parenting adolescents at this time is much more difficult. Many things are coming against young people that cannot be seen without spiritual discernment. Consider that there may be a purpose for their lives that may not necessarily fit our plan. God has a plan for their lives just like He has one for us. We must pray, "God's will be done" for this is the perfect prayer. We must be careful that we are not forcing *our* will on *their* lives.

Watching my children move from teens into adulthood was difficult because I had it all planned out. Yes, I was that controlling mom. But over time, I had to learn that they had to make their own choices and mistakes. It was surely difficult for me to watch. I only wish I had known more about having difficult conversations that may have helped them dispel some of the lies the enemy was speaking to them. I wish I had known how to better pray for them and teach them how to build a personal relationship with God. But God provides. Despite my failures, they have turned out well and know the love of God.

Judges 14:4 "His father and mother didn't realize the LORD was at work in this, creating an opportunity to work against the Philistines, who ruled over Israel at that time."

Chapter 7
Wilderness Wanderings

"Every branch in me that beareth not fruit he taketh away: and every branch that beareth fruit, he purgeth it, that it may bring forth more fruit." John 15:2

I heard Bishop TD Jakes say in one of his sermons, "Anytime God does something for you, and you don't have a point of reference, it is frightening. There are times in life when God doesn't care about your comfort. Sometimes you have to be uncomfortable." Our time I describe as the wilderness season, was certainly an uncomfortable time, but I am assured that it was still God's plan.

After Corion was released from the specialty hospital into rehab, we were forced more than ever to walk by faith and not by sight. I didn't understand many things we experienced at that time. Being who I am, I mostly wondered why we were going through so much. I didn't feel adequate nor equipped to handle where we were in our lives. I didn't know what I was doing or what needed to be done.

I often wished there was a book or manual that would tell us what to do. We had to trust in those placed in our path and often just go on pure instinct from God's leading to find answers. It was definitely like wandering in the wilderness for many years.

I used the research skills I developed over the years at my job to find things that would help him get back on his feet. I believe the limitations of care had more to do with his insurance than anything else. Even when I wanted to find physical therapy options that we could pay for out of pocket, there were still obstacles. I definitely tried all that I knew, but it was always met with much resistance. But it never stopped me from trying again.

Nonetheless, God led us step-by-step. At each step, God guided us. He placed the people we needed in place just as we needed. We got to a point where the nurses would ask me if I worked in healthcare. I would tell them, "No, I'm a mother and a banker". God gave me the wisdom I needed each step of the way.

I am truly grateful to one of the female doctors that corrected me when I started my sentence off with, "I'm not a doctor, but..." She said, "Hold up. Let me correct you. You *are* his doctor. You know more about him than we do. So please tell me whatever it is you think I need to know." That helped build my confidence when speaking to the professionals because I was with him at just about every medical visit.

God makes provision for what needs to happen. You don't have to have it all figured out, as a matter of fact, most times, you won't. And if you are so tied to your plans, you will be frustrated and want to give up. I know I did. You have to give up control and trust God. He already knows your ability. I had to learn not to be distracted by the *how*. God will make a way. Faith is believing when you don't see it. It's knowing God has a plan no matter how things appear.

The Purging

When I think of purging, I think of the removal of someone or something. To reconcile the notion of people not caring enough to be present, I consider that maybe God removed those who could not handle this season of the journey. I thought certain people would be there with us through the hard places, but they just were not.

I remember telling my sister Crystal several years into the process, "If Corion passes away, I am not going to let anyone know because they should have been there." I am honest enough to say that I was angry because I felt like so many people abandoned him and me in a time of need.

He asked me once in the car, coming home from church, "*Where they at? Where everybody at?*" So, I had to console him with this revelation, "Corion, in life there are people that need you and people that you need. Once you cannot give the people who need you what they desire, they will get their needs met through someone else. But those people you need are here. We will show them our love and appreciate them more."

We were surrounded by the people we needed. Their presence was always felt in times of need. We may have felt lonely or by ourselves many times, but we were always surrounded by love and the presence of the Holy Spirit. I'm assured of that.

I can recall in the scripture where the Lord told Gideon he had too many soldiers. The word also only calls for two or three to gather, and He promises to be in the mist. When God is in control, it only takes a few. We had all that we needed. And as I look back, there were only a few at one time, but overall there were many. Everyone intended for the journey had their time and space.

The Pruning

The Lord was with us, but it doesn't mean it felt this way all the time. You can't figure out what this season means while you are still in it. You must choose to see it that way. How will you interpret the losing season of your life? We always assume it is a punishment because we know our sins. He is pruning you in the process so that you can be even more fruitful. (John 15:2)

The wilderness season is intended to grow our faith. God will use the pressures of life to bring you into the freedom He has for you. I was used to being in control and planning every moment of my life. But I clearly recall the Holy Spirit asking me while I was sitting in the waiting room of the hospital in 2014, "Who told you, you were Jesus?" Ashamed, I acknowledged, "I guess I told myself that." Saying you trust God is easy. But to know you truly trust God is trusting Him when He is all you have.

If you always think it's the devil attacking you, you will miss the opportunity to bear fruit. Stay connected to the true vine. Ask God what it means. The saints would say, just go through. I couldn't understand that until now. The proof is in the pruning.

But in this season, I first had to learn the difference between the enemy and the voice of God. God was teaching us His love while I was misinterpreting the season. I've since come to understand that the intentions of the enemy do not control our life. It's easier said than done, but I had to learn how to stand against the wiles (schemes) of the enemy.

The Branches

05/10/19 (social media post)

WARNING LONG POST!!! Today I'm having another "Why Lord?" moment. I ask this when I just don't understand why we are here in this moment. Why we keep going thru the same issues and circumstances with no clear end or cure. And in my moment, I thought about people that I have encountered along this journey. And the fact that it is nurse's week. I think about Stacy Leigh Bisignano who met Corion before this tragedy and appreciate her patience and care for him while we dealt with my mother in the ICU. She still follows us and prays for us. I love you, Stacy. I think about the many nurses we've met in the ICU with him the following week and the weeks thereafter, especially the one that encouraged me to take my time in making a decision to remove him from life support. I think about the one nurse that asked me if I was okay and if I understood the gravity of the moment as if she didn't have any faith in the same God I was trusting in for a miracle. I just believed that He did it for her. I then think upon the many many nurses that have held my hand and wiped my tears at the hospital visits, nursing facilities, dialysis centers, and my FAVORITE group, Interventional Nephrology on Union. A few that stand out most are Kim, Erica, John and Timarako. You have a place in our hearts that can never be removed. And I would be remiss not to mention the countless CNAs (Lisa, Candi, Ms. Pat, Terrell Akins, MeMe and Bobby) that are more like family and friends than caregivers. Maybe meeting you all is a reason for the journey. Undoubtedly our paths may have never been crossed otherwise. I'm probably still going to have "Why Lord" moments, but

I am thankful that you all have been here to help us as we move towards the answer. HAPPY NURSES WEEK!!

This post reminds me of the many branches God added to our life. Many were "cut away", but for everyone that left, God added more. I quickly learned that family isn't always the ones that will be by your side in times of trouble. Felt like the people I was closest to and thought would support us just wasn't the case. But even with that, I learned to depend on the help of strangers, and more importantly, how to ask for help.

Asking for help was an area I wasn't familiar with and where I needed help with most. I developed a new muscle in learning to be vulnerable. It allowed me to get the support I needed from others and allowed my family, especially my husband, to see a side of me that he hadn't experienced before.

When you are always expected, or perceived, to be the "strong" one, then it takes some getting used to in showing vulnerability. I have since learned that I don't have to do everything. I've folded up my "superwoman cape" and put it in the back of the closet.

Trying to be everything for everyone isn't realistic for me anymore. I do what I can for who I can, but I learned to save my best for my immediate family. That's who will suffer most when I am gone, so I will give them the best of me now, as well as save some for myself. Self-love is required.

I recall a special moment when my husband encouraged me to take care of myself. He said, "You are the glue that holds all this together. If you fall apart, the whole thing falls." Then not only did he encourage me, but he also actually put action behind it. He made sure he was with me every step of the way, insisted that we get away to decompress, and supported all of my crazy ideas as we worked to care for Corion.

The Scrubbing Process

This season was the beginning of the scrubbing process. God was scrubbing the stains and changing my perspective, so I could see Him more clearly. I was in the wilderness of becoming. God wants to dwell on the inside, and He will drive you into His presence through discomfort.

I began this journey thinking I had control over my life, and not just my life but the lives of my children and my husband. See, it's that word "my" that gets us into the wrong character. I had to learn that God blessed me with the people in my life to help me along this journey. My children have taught me unconditional love, my husband has taught me how to receive love even if it doesn't look like what I expect. And friends and family have taught me that I am not alone.

Circumstances of life had hardened my heart, made me self-reliant, and made me afraid to love freely. I experienced disappointment, abandonment, sexual abuse, and rejection. But even in that, I had experienced a level of love but other people's issues covered it up.

God used this journey to heal me in all those places. I learned a level of love, respect, honor, and awareness that I didn't know before. I am able to meet people where they are and not try to make them be who I need them to be for me. I want others to know that God will take your brokenness and create a beautiful story of love. He will meet your deepest need.

Chapter 8
Our Walk Thru the Valley

Fear thou not; for I am with thee: be not dismayed; for I am thy God: I will strengthen thee; yea, I will help thee; yea, I will uphold thee with the right hand of my righteousness. Isaiah 41:10

To make it to the next level, you must first master the low places. Let that sink in. The aggression Corion exhibited bothered me the most. I didn't want him to hurt anyone, and I certainly did not want anyone to hurt him.

I've always tried to remain positive and of good cheer, but, as I'm sure you can imagine, there were many low places, or valley moments, along the journey. During the span of 90 days, from Corion's injury, we lost my mother and a brother-in-law. In January of the next year, my husband's brother sustained a head injury as well. He is doing well in recovery.

Corion's memory was greatly affected by the brain injury. In the beginning, it seemed that he was progressing beautifully. But after all of the medication and time, it seemed he started to regress. He didn't know who we were, couldn't remember our names, and was just so angry all of the time.

It was difficult at times accepting that he may not remember that I am his mother. He would say, *"You not my damn mother."* So, I began to tell him, "Well, just consider me your friend because I'm not going anywhere." He called most of the women that cared for him "Mother" and some other choice words. He eventually began to accept that I was "the mother".

We would practice everyone's name and who they were to him. It was frustrating for him, of course. It was always a joy when he would be able to remember someone without any prompting from me. He never forgot his name and his birthday. He eventually began to remember the names of the family members, his address, phone number, city, and state.

One of the hardest things to do was constantly employ someone to sit with him at dialysis. When Cory was with him during the first several months, he would sit with him and ensure he didn't pull his needles out. Corion exhibited extreme aggression and confusion.

After Cory had to leave, I worked with a series of sitters. At first, I was able to use some CNAs that cared for him at the nursing facility. My sister Crystal & her friends, my in-laws, and a few of Corion's friends pitched in to help. But anytime there was a problem, I was the point of contact. I had to leave work to run back and forth to the dialysis center much too often.

One day on my way there, I cried out to God and said, please remove this burden. I can deal with everything else if you could please just provide me someone consistent. He did just that. Ms. Pat came on board soon after his other long-time sitter Candi. Ms. Pat was so dependable and good with him. She sat with him for almost 3 years, up until he stopped dialysis.

Finding solutions to problems was equally as frustrating. You would think the people that work in healthcare could at least direct you to the places and people with the answers. Well, that is just not true. At least it certainly wasn't for our situation. I spent most of my days figuring out who to call and who can help with each issue that came up. I know he wasn't the first person to have this type of injury and surely not the last. I hope that I can find a way to be a resource for others in the future.

Nursing care was not a good experience either. In fact, it was what I spent most of my tears on. When you don't truly care about people, you should definitely not work in this field. I've seen enough lack of concern and neglect to last me the rest of my life.

There were many days I cried because I felt like I didn't have a better choice. I could have chosen something different, but I wasn't sure if quitting my job and staying home to care for him on my own was the answer. The times I did explore the option, God just didn't confirm that it was what I was supposed to do.

So, I chose to use the nursing system and work to be with him as much as possible. I am thankful to God for sending the caregivers that cared along the journey. At our last facility, we developed some rapport with many that I felt had his best interest at heart as much as they could. But it was always a source of contention.

The greatest valley moments had to do with his behavior issues. I didn't mind the feeding and the changing, but the cussing and fighting almost took me out on several occasions. I cried constantly about this. And when Corion came home during the pandemic, it was just me and him most of the time.

He was "team too much" on many occasions. I contemplated taking him back to the nursing home many times, but I knew it would be even harder not being able to see him. So, I just had to suck it up and see what the Lord had for me to learn from this foolishness.

Journal Entry 06/20/20

One morning during my quiet time with God, he told me, "This is you when things don't go your way." When it doesn't happen the way you thought it would or in your mind should have gone down, you get disappointed and don't want to move forward because you don't want to be disappointed any further. Then you try to act as though you don't care or make your feelings numb to what is happening. You start wishing for it to just be all over so you can move on to something else and no longer think about this thing.

I also wrote down, "an unexpected end" in the middle of the conversation. Then, you start blaming yourself and practicing how you would have done things differently and if it would have been a different outcome. You start practicing how you will tell the story because you have written the ending. Does anyone else do this, or is it just me? Am I being prideful?

Nineveh comes to mind. The city was proud, and God judged them. Jonah tried to go the opposite way from where the Lord was leading him because he had already written the ending of the story before he became obedient to God. Peter said that he wouldn't deny Jesus, but he denied the Lord three times before the cock crowed. Maybe this is pride disguised as disappointment.

I didn't find the word disappointment in the Bible. In my research, the definitions are in many ways the same because disappointment can be the result of pride. We must submit to God's plan. His thoughts are not our thoughts. His ways are not our ways.

We must remember that God's plan has already accounted for what we are concerned about. We are in uncharted territories. Our lives are not like someone else's life. Our path is our path and connected to another life, so we can't control all of the encounters or outcomes.

We can renew our minds and consider these things as part of the process and a new experience that will lead to another amazing victory in Jesus. The word says, "Be ye also ready." I try to stay ready because the spirit of the Lord will take over my conversation at any moment. I must be sure I am walking in His way so that I may be used by the spirit to continue the work that has been placed within me.

It is my prayer that other's experiences of Corion serve to edify the body of Christ and to give glory to God's plan. I pray that nothing he has done or said hindered God's plans for his life. I pray that I cannot disguise pridefulness as disappointment with God's plan.

God's way is a process and not a problem to be resolved. It requires a renewing of your mind. Pulling down strongholds requires renewing of the mind. For his yoke is easy and his burden is light. But wisdom is proved right by *her deeds. No one knows the Son except the Father, and no one knows the Father except the Son and those to whom the Son chooses to reveal him.*

Matthew 28 and 30 says, "Come to me all you who are weary and burdened, and I will give you rest. Take my yoke upon you and learn from me, for I am gentle and humble in heart, and you will find rest for your souls. For my yoke is easy and my burden is light."

For the light speaks to the renewing of your mind. God shines a different light on my burden that lessened the fear of disappointment or facing issues because He has already lifted those burdens. His plan is perfect. I'm just an instrument in his orchestra. I can recall riding in my car talking to the Lord and He spoke to me and said, "Do not be dismayed." I later looked up that scripture to find that it also says that he will help me. I am so grateful that God has not been slack in His promises towards me.

I have learned that God will walk with you and feed you through the low places. When we learn to change our conversation to praise, we can shift in our situation. Praise confuses the enemy; that's the secret. We must change words. If we change our words, we can change our perspective. We must learn to say, "He did it FOR me" instead of "to me".

02/04/17 (social media post)
God said to me, "Don't be dismayed by the process. I am God." Then I read Isiah 42:10. SMH. It was for me, but I don't mind sharing.

Chapter 9

His Healing

"For my thoughts are not your thoughts, neither are your ways my ways, saith the Lord." Isaiah 55:8

Early on in our journey, I began to post updates to Facebook for family and friends. I wanted all to experience the miracle we were witnessing. I tagged most of my posts with the hashtag #watchGodwork and #prayerworks. I am so happy that God gave me the foresight to do this because it has allowed me to go back and see where we have been.

In revisiting past posts, I can see where Corion's physical healing began. Looking at pictures, videos, and posts, I can see that God healed Corion in the same year. He began breathing on his own in February, moving his arms and legs, and by March, he was trying to speak, asking for prayer, ice, and snacks.

Facebook posts:

01/26/2014

This morning Robert and I woke up to Corion Reed gagging and in distress. It was really hard to see. But after they finally got him calm the nurse says thank God cause that means he is coming back this way. I PRAISE and

THANK GOD for His wondrous and mighty acts! MTC can I get somebody anybody to take off running around that church for ME!

01/31/2014

Just got to the hospital. My boy, Corion Reed, looking sooooo good. I'm told he is breathing better against the machine and his eyes are bright. But most of all I can tell he is trying to squeeze my hand. The prayers of the righteous availeth much! God thank you and praise you for the sign. God is an AWESOME and FAITHFUL God!!!!

02/13/2014

Yall ain't gone believe this but Thank God I got a witness. I asked Corion Reed to blink if he love me and he wouldn't. I was messing with him, asking how you gone do me like that. I told him I love him anyway and bent down to kiss him and HE KISSED ME!! Robert said yep I saw it. He kissed you! My God is AWESOME!

02/18/2014

Guess what? Corion Reed has been breathing on his own for the past 4 hours. Oh what a mighty God we serve. Keep praying for you are in the midst of a miracle.

03/05/2014

Last night I had a conversation with Corion Dshawn Reed. Yes I said CONVERSATION!! I couldn't understand every word, but I understood enough to know how he is feeling and that he wanted some ICE!! The Lord is AMAZING and so worthy to be PRAISED!! I don't know about you, but

GOD is truly taking me to another place through this experience. I have a much greater understanding each day of TRULY TRUSTING GOD. LORD I TRUST YOU!! I admonish you today to put your trust in GOD; not in man, jobs, things, circumstances, or even in yourself too much. Trust God!

04/20/2014

Determined, Fighter, Blessed. All these words describe Corion Reed. Amazing, Faithful, Merciful. All these words describe the God we serve. With the help of the Lord alone he fed himself a sandwich today. And JACORI recorded it....priceless!

04/21/2014

Corion Reed drank from a cup today by himself. Won't HE do it. He had witnesses too!

05/23/2014

PRAISE REPORT!! The Occupational Therapist for Corion called ME this evening EXCITED about his progress. She said he is throwing the basketball in the net and made the shot three times; he is sitting up on the edge of the bed unassisted and will put his socks on with assistance. I was so happy to hear the excitement and hope in her voice. Today marks exactly 4 months. Will you PRAISE GOD for His goodness and keeping power with me?!

06/21/2014

Corion I'm told he wanted a snack, and no one was in the room. So you know what he did right?! Got himself out of bed and onto the floor to get his Cheetos and M&Ms. Lord have mercy! Corion told the nurse when she came in that he "wanted it". This boy will be independent once again!

06/29/2014

Corion knew Jacori when he came in! And J said "daddy" and he said "Huh"? Had to be priceless for J cause it definitely was for me!

08/01/2014

Y'all (yeah I said it) I just spent the afternoon with Corion in dialysis and in his words "we had fun in there". We laughed, played a game on my tablet, and ate snacks. He said to the ladies 'running' (he mean walking) and standing that they need to say thank you. They didn't understand but truly I did cause he admires the fact that they can stand and walk and doesn't understand yet why he can't "get up". He also told me that I'm not his mother (I hear it all the time) but I took off my glasses and he said I kind of look like her "fo real tho". And we changed my name today to 'mama'. I am thoroughly enjoying our time together. Have a blessed Friday Faces!

Our Healing

God's ways and plans are strategic. Our lives and blessings are not just about us. There is always a greater plan that we are not fully aware of, tied to the blessing of others. Corion's healing and the process were not just about Corion. His healing and this journey are tied to the healing of many.

Healing was extended to our family through this journey with Corion and others who came in contact with him. My husband and I were at a crossroad in our marriage when his illness began. Our journey with

Corion helped us to put many things into perspective. I recall a day we had him home, and it is as if he was fully aware of the conflict between us. But he told me, *"Forgive that mane, he sorry."* I decided to do just that.

I'm sure he probably had his own personal conversation with Robert as well. We were able to resolve our differences and see a bigger picture. Our relationship is much bigger than ourselves. It is our legacy for our children, grandchildren and those that come after us. Our marriage became stronger, and love grew deeper while we worked as a team through this journey.

As a stronger unit, our family experienced a season of healing and bonding. We were intentional about spending more time together, creating special moments and making as many memories as possible. We now know how precious time is, and we didn't know how much time we had with him. We made a point to take family portraits for Christmas that first year and several years after. We have many photos and videos to capture as many memories as possible over the years we had together.

Cory was able to come to Memphis and spend a great deal of time caring for him. He was able to solidify the relationship with him that he had not had in years past. This also allowed him to develop a relationship with his grandson, Jacori. Even he and Robert could garner a friendship that allowed us all the ability to work together to help Corion as he began to heal.

My sister Crystal and Corion were like siblings, as well as best friends. She would come to town often, just to not miss out on the birthday parties, trips, and joyous moments with the family. The bond they built continues to flow down to her great-niece and nephews. This level of love and relationship is important and truly needed for this younger generation.

Corion found so much joy in spending time with his nephew and later niece. I remember the time in the rehab when he asked where Danielle was. He wanted to see her. After she made it there, he touched her belly to signify that he understood that she was still pregnant with Jace at the time. Jace had the opportunity to build a lasting bond with his beloved Uncle. Aria was afraid of him at first, but she soon got used to him and would fuss as if he was the child and she was the big sister. I am certain it meant a lot to Danielle that her children had the opportunity to know her big brother and personal bodyguard.

As for me, I was given the opportunity to spend more time with my son to bind up some old wounds we had developed. All the time, fights, and memories we were able to share will shape the rest of my life. My journey with Corion helped me learn more about myself and build a stronger relationship with the Lord. I am forever affected and grateful for our time together.

Chapter 10

It's Cheap, It's Easy, It's Free

"Who will have all men to be saved, and to come unto the knowledge of the truth. For there is one God, and one mediator between God and men, the man Christ Jesus; Who gave himself a ransom for all, to be testified in due time." 1 Timothy 2:4-6

If you picked up this book to see if you can be "convinced" that God is real, then I pray this is enough at this point to encourage you to confess with your mouth and believe in your heart that Christ died on the cross for your sins. God is ready and willing to lead and guide you just as He has for us. He is here with you, right now, just open up your heart to Him. He knows your name, He hears your prayers, He even knows every hair on your head. You don't have to earn his love. He already loves you.

Repentance is not only about turning away from sin, but it is also about turning to God and His will for our lives. Say this prayer with me, Forgive me Lord. I am sorry that I have sinned against you. I confess with my mouth and believe in my heart that your son Christ Jesus died so that I may be saved. Come into my life and my heart. Please lead and guide me and direct me in the way you wish for me to go, so that your plan for my life may be fulfilled.

If you accept this offer of salvation, take some time to thank God for this wonderful gift.

My son would tell me random things when I would enter his room, especially during the week he transitioned. One thing he said was, *"It's cheap, it's easy, it's free."* I shared this with my good friend, Iris, and she said, "That's salvation." My spirit leaped listening to this revelation.

We've heard for years that salvation is free. It is easy because it is a confession and change of mind. Some may argue that it isn't cheap because there is a cost in giving up the things you used to do. However, when compared to the promises of God, its value is immeasurable and doesn't cost you a thing.

God's love is like the love of a grandmother; you don't have to earn it. She already loves you unconditionally. But when you do wrong, she corrects you in love and guides you with her wisdom from years of life experiences.

After Corion's passing, the Holy Spirit told me, the people on this journey with us, his circle, are God's disciples, and they are to share His word. They must first work to cultivate a personal relationship with God, repent of any sin, forgive whoever you need to forgive, confess that Christ died for your sins and ask for salvation. Corion said, it's cheap, it's easy and it's free.

Jesus wants everyone to be ready to meet him at his appearing. I was sure to tell as many of them as I could while they were standing still enough to listen. God told me to say, "He's coming, He's coming, He's coming." I am here to sound the alarm. He is coming!

What Happened Next?

So, you decided to read on. Good, I was hoping you would. I wanted to be sure to get the opportunity for salvation out early for those who may not be as interested in the conclusion of the matter. I am also convinced that we should usher in the presence of God when we discuss some matters that may become a bit unnerving for some. And for those that are not yet convinced that God is real, I'm happy you are here.

My sincere prayer is that through Corion's journey, you may be able to see how God revealed himself and used this young man to teach our family unconditional love, the value of time, and strengthened our faith through the power of prayer.

There were many layers to this six-year battle with an anoxic brain injury coupled with a prior diagnosis of end-stage renal failure. There were many frustrating days with the healthcare industry, a lot of loneliness and uncertainty while still holding on to faith and genuine hope in Christ.

This story may not flow in chronological order because, in hindsight, I am able to see things from a different perspective. I've always known that we were a living witness to a miracle, but it was not until the end that God revealed how faithful He is to His word.

Thank you for taking this ride with us. I pray that you are as blessed by his life as we have been.

Chapter 11
"I heard my daddy's voice"

"Don't let anyone look down on you because you are young, but set an example for the believers in speech, in conduct, in love, in faith and in purity." 1 Timothy 4:12

Jacori was only six years old when this all happened. We weren't sure how he would handle it or even what to tell him. We debated allowing  him to see his Dad on the ventilator in the hospital for the first time. We were afraid that memory would scar him. But we considered it could be a moment for him to say his goodbyes, or give Corion the strength to pull through. So we decided as a family to allow him to see him.

He was such a trooper. I can remember him saying, "I'm going to miss him." He took it like a champ, with no tears or questions. Later, when we moved to the step-down hospital, Jacori got excited at the sound of Corion coughing after the trach had

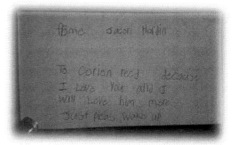

been removed. He said, "Gigi, I heard my daddy's voice!" He was so eager to hear it again that he placed his hand on his father and prayed for him. He even wrote him a letter that I saved for Corion to have when he woke up. It read, "To Corion Reed, because I love you and I will love him more, just please wake up."

God answered this baby's prayer. At the end of 2014, our family was able to do a photo shoot. Time was precious, and while we still had our

miracle with us, we wanted to capture every moment. I was surprised to find the sign I had purchased the year before that said, "Believe in Miracles". We were so fortunate to use that sign and capture a precious moment with *our* miracle.

We will one day know the long-term effects these moments have had on such a young child. From watching him today, they have been mostly positive. I can imagine he will have some struggles about losing his dad. However, I truly believe that the love surrounding him and his faith in our Lord will sustain him. I look forward to him becoming a strong man, just like his dad.

Over the years, he has been able to have some precious memories. His dad has been to a couple of his games, he has been able to play ball with him, and he even scolded him about his bad grades once.

While riding to church, I told Corion that Jacori made an F on his report card. Corion said, *"An F!"* Then he turned to me and asked, *"That's not good is it, ma?"* I said no it isn't. He then told him *"I know you are smart. I know you can do better."* Then with much concern, he asked his middle schooler, *"Do you know your ABC's?"* We tried so hard not to laugh. It was such a priceless memory for us all.

Jacori told me once, "I don't care how my dad is, I just want him to live." His mom, Jasmine, always ensured that he spent as much time as he wanted with him. My husband and I would have Corion home on weekends to spend the night with his son for family time. Jacori dancing while Corion was his hype man are the best memories for me.

Watching Jacori with his dad has been so sweet. He has helped me feed him, get him dressed, help lift him, and he even made breakfast for him before he headed to dialysis once. They would spend lots of time laughing, watching tv, listening to music and eating cookies, which everyone knows was Corion's favorite snack during this time.

The smiles and laughter said enough. Though only time will tell of the impact of these past six years on this young soul, I am certain the level of compassion he will have for the disabled will be immeasurable.

Daddy God

Today, when I hear the voice of our Father in Heaven, it fills me with excitement and an eagerness to do His will. During this journey, I heard the voice of my Daddy God say to my spirit, "You are my daughter." That still fills me with so much joy. I long to hear His voice daily, just as Jacori did for his daddy.

God will respond openly to our secret conversations with Him (prayers). I've experienced this time and time again. The response for me would come through someone that knows nothing of my prayer. There will be something about the prayer that a sermon or even conversation will speak to, and I know it is the voice of God.

The scripture in John 10:27 tells us, "My sheep hear my voice, and I know them, and they follow me." I know my husband's truck when it turns on our street, even before it pulls into the driveway. I listen for it at night and say to myself with a cheerful heart, "here comes my husband." At first, I would mistake the car next door for his truck. Soon I learned to tell the two apart. God spoke to me one of those nights and challenged me to know His voice the way I know Robert's truck coming up the street. Wow! I've been working on that skill ever since.

A Parent's Voice

In the ER, on the day of Corion's heart failure, he could still hear my voice. The nurse confirmed that they got a pulse for the first time when I called his name upon entering the room. Just as a mother knows the voice of her child amongst a crowd of crying babies, so does that child know the voice of their mother. Even after Corion returned to us, he could hear my voice before I entered a room. He would yell out, "Momma", before I could get to him.

His hearing was so strong, and we often called it supernatural. He could hear us speaking even if we were in another room. Robert and I would often find ourselves whispering in the kitchen to keep him from hearing our conversations. LOL. The voice of a parent is powerful. It has lasting effects on the child.

If we consistently tell our children that they are beautiful, powerful, and loved from an early age, then maybe they won't go out seeking and finding the wrong version of this love, power, and beauty. During his illness, Corion would often ask me, *"Do you love me Ma?"* Lord how can this child doubt my love for him? I got a second chance that everyone doesn't get to dispel the myth within him that I didn't love him.

Many times, the enemy begins to tell us lies about ourselves at an early age. Then these lies play over and over in our little minds until they become how we see ourselves. But those lies are planted to keep us from discovering who we truly are and how God sees us.

I wrote a list of affirmations for Corion and put it on his wall after he kept telling me about what he can't do. He would say that he didn't have a brain anymore and that he didn't know anything. He kept using defeating phrases. I wrote this to remind him that he was an overcomer, and that God was always with him.

As parents, we must always be careful of the conversations and words we pour into our children. They will believe what we say, and often, we will be the only ones that can convince them otherwise. Our words and tone are powerful, and we must begin to choose them more wisely. I've made many mistakes with my voice and my words. I have been working overtime trying to undo the damage.

I remember when Corion came to dialysis extremely upset. There must have been a conversation someone was having in his presence, and I believe he assumed they were talking about him. He said, *"They called me stupid!"* Since he didn't understand his brain injury, he most likely related to this inadequacy, but he was extremely angry and adamant that he was not stupid.

I had to tell him often that he was highly intelligent. He didn't understand his condition, but as I continuously told him how blessed, handsome, strong, and amazing he was, he soon started to believe it for himself. It built his confidence. It gave him the strength he would need to continue in the fight.

In that same way he strengthened me. He told me that God loved me, that God knows that I am a winner. He said that I am *a beautiful mother*, and he said that I am *very incredible*. But most of all, he said many times, *"I'm proud of you ma!"* That means so much to me, even more now than ever before.

Wow! All my life I have looked for these types of reassurances. The devil stole my confidence at an early age. I tried to overcompensate through knowledge and intelligence because I knew I had that from my accomplishments in school. That was undeniable, but it didn't completely help my confidence.

I believe when God says in Matthew 6:33, he'll add things to you, those things are not only material things, but also spiritual riches. I needed the confidence to move forward in this journey and for the purpose God has placed within me. He added intangible needs (things) to us both throughout our journey.

God will work things out together for the good of those who love him and diligently seek Him. God's love is gentle and kind, and He loves us just the way we are and not how the world has created us to believe ourselves to be.

His love doesn't have to be earned. He knew us before we were placed in our mother's womb. The scripture tells us that He blew His breath in us, so He is already inside of us. There is a gift inside of you just waiting to get out, but in order to fully benefit from the gift, you must seek out the truth of God through His word.

You must not continue to believe the lies of the enemy and what he says about you. You are fearfully and wonderfully made.

Psalms 139:13-14 - For you created my inmost being; you knit me together in my mother's womb. I praise you because I am fearfully and wonderfully made; your works are wonderful; I know that full well.

Protecting Our Children

When Corion first started talking clearly again, he angrily said, *"Leave the kids alone! Why y'all messing with the kids!"* It struck me as strange at the time because there were no kids around. We were in the nursing home. He was extremely angry about something he could see that we could not see.

He also asked for Danielle. She was pregnant at the time. I called her and when she made it there, he placed his hand on her stomach as if he was praying for the unborn child. I was amazed that he remembered that she was pregnant. She told him, "Yea the baby still in there."

Another interesting fact is that one of the nurses that cared for him for quite a while at the facility was pregnant. I had been informed about him having several behavioral issues, so I was quite surprised to see her caring for him alone. I expressed my concern for her, but she assured me that he never gave her any problems. He was protective of children just as he had always been.

We must take the time to pray often for the protection of our children from dangers seen and unseen. There are many evils present in the world today and it is up to us as adults to protect their innocence from spiritual wickedness. I heard in the spirit that things are coming against our children that we are not aware of. We must stay vigilant and mindful of this fact.

Let us begin to consistently pray that the Father reveals to us deep and hidden things, for He knows what lies in darkness, and light dwells with Him. The devil can't stand up against the word of God. Let's pray…

Heavenly Father,
We come to you asking that you protect and shield our children from dangers seen and unseen. We ask that you cover and keep them under your divine protection that they may be able to live out your purpose and plan for their lives. God go before them and cancel every assignment of the enemy against their lives. We plead the blood of Jesus over our children, ourselves, families, friends, and communities. We give you all the glory, honor and praise. It's in your son Jesus name that we do ask these things in prayer.
AMEN

Chapter 12

Abundant Life

"The thief cometh not, but for to steal, and to kill, and to destroy: I am come that they might have life, and that they might have it more abundantly." John 10:10

My kids used to stay up all night during the summer in the late '90s and early 2000 just to watch **Good Times**. They loved **Good Times**. Since this had been a favorite pastime for Corion, I imagined that it may bring about some comfort and great memories, so I purchased the series on DVD. I was right. He remembered the song and even after a while, remembered many of the episodes. But he wasn't very fond of some of the outcomes and got mad at *JJ and Thelma* when they would argue and fight. It was as if he was in the house with them. Many times, I would have to turn it off because he would get so agitated.

He liked a few more shows like **Martin** and his favorite was **Fresh Prince**. I bought those DVDs as well. I just wanted him to remember the good times he had with his family. I wanted him to remember that we used to laugh and that he was loved.

Our Travels

During this journey, we tried to create new memories as well. Our first visit home, our trips to visit church and family on Sunday in Byhalia, Mississippi, and even some overnight stays at home were all great. We took a trip to Nashville twice to see Jacori, his son, play ball.

We got adventurous and did an overnight trip with our family to the waterpark in Arkansas. And as if that weren't ambitious enough, we did a weekend trip to Atlanta, Georgia. Initially, it was for my class reunion, but it soon took on a mind of its own, and just became a mission to get him on the road to see his 80-year-old grandmother and Uncle Chuck. It turned out to be a great vacation for him.

Celebrations

We always celebrated holidays, the anniversary of his rebirth and his birthday, especially since it was Christmas Day. I've always tried to make birthdays special. It's a tradition I inherited from my mom.

We celebrated his Dirty Thirty (30th) birthday bash with a few friends and family. He had such a wonderful time. I am so grateful for many friends of me and Crystal who helped with decorations. All guests came in their 90's attire dressed for the occasion. Danielle did a great job with the music and my Keke always comes through with the food. His faithful few friends showed up and even his dad, my best friend and her son, Malik came in from Atlanta. It was truly a great time. The miracle of it all was that Corion had been in the hospital days before and came out just in time for the party.

His presence at my surprise birthday party when I turned 50 just made it so much more special. We were always cautious about taking him to unfamiliar places and around a lot of people. He could be a bit anxious and loud. But that night he was simply amazing and enjoyed every moment. They truly surprised me and Corion being there was the best part for me. My family, friends and support team are simply the BEST!

The most memorable party for me was me and Robert's 25th Wedding Anniversary celebration where Corion pretty much stole the show, just as he had always done before. That was truly a great time. We danced and took photos. His sitter, Pat, said he realized he was someplace different because of the food. It was an awesome night.

We would always celebrate the anniversary of his rebirth, Jan 23rd of each year by doing something special, especially playing basketball. I'd take him to the community center for the disabled to shoot some hoops. He loved that! When I wanted to get out, I could always count on Terrell to escort us to doctor's visits and other outings. He and I took Corion to the mall one year. I remembered that Corion had asked his cousin, Miles to take him when he visited early on. When we got there, he said, *"I feel like running."* We laughed because we knew that we would probably run too if he did.

I generally created a theme for each year during this time. Our theme for 2017 was Back to Living and it turned out to be his best year health-wise. That was the year we only had to go into the hospital once. That was considered a great year, especially when compared to the years that followed. My goal was to create a better quality of life despite all the challenges he faced. On the last anniversary of his rebirth, we had a conversation.

> *01/23/20 (social media post*
> *I've been feeling melancholy all day, but his face and his words*
> *always get me through. "I came back because I have something to do. I*
> *know what I gotta do."* He said to me, *"You've done*
> *everything you were supposed to do, and it's been good."*

I cling to those words now because I sometimes feel like I should have done more. Many times during his stay at home, he would say in a sarcastic tone, *"are you still having fun,"* especially when he was being a complete jerk. Then he would say, *"This ain't fun mama. You think this fun? This ain't fun."* He would even mock me and ask, *"you still love Corion? I love Corion. I love Corion"*. I can laugh at it now, but it would really get under my skin at the time.

I was doing all I could to make sure he was comfortable, safe, clean, well-fed and having fun. But there was no more I could do. It wasn't fun. His biggest complaint was that he couldn't have sex. He was soooo angry about that, which I completely understood seeing he was still a young man. He just wanted me to understand why he was coming to the conclusion he knew was imminent, and I get it now.

We made many great memories as a family especially for his son. His nephew and niece had a chance to enjoy his presence as well. But before he transitioned, he let me know that the kids were not going to understand. But he said, *"I need to do this, and I want to do this."* He was ready to exchange this life for another life, everlasting life.

His Smile

The nurse at rehab told me that Corion may never smile again because he had to access a different area of his brain that sustained damage. But God! He got his smile back the same year!

03/13/2014 (post)
I've been waiting to exhale for 50 days! And today, I see the sunshine amongst the clouds. As one of Corion Dshawn Reed's favorite songs says "A change is gonna come…oh yes it will." The nurses were about to move him last night when I came in. I went over to see what he was saying, and he said, "Pray for me". You know I did right! JESUS! And he almost showed us a smile when he saw his aunt Ericka Hayes. Today he will be moving on to his next level of care at a local rehab. Thank you for your continued prayers! Have a blessed day!

Psalm 110:3b "….and your strength shall be renewed day by day like morning dew."

03/31/2014
Good morning FBFam! Hope you all had a wonderful weekend. I just wanted to share one thing that excited me yesterday and I almost forgot because of a more pressing situation. Corion SMILED!! Yes he gave me a smile yesterday. I asked him to do it again and again and he did. That boy is truly a FIGHTER, and our God is so AMAZING! HE consistently reminds us that HE will answer our prayers and that HE is in control. Give God control of your situation today. HE can handle it! Trust HIM! Have a blessed day FBFam!

Psalm 31:14-15 ESV
"But I trust in you, O Lord; I say, "You are my God." My times are in your hand"

08/03/2016 (social media post)
Kidney failure, brain injury, so many vascath replacement procedures we lost count, permacath in neck, mercer infection, bile issues, no food since 6p yesterday, restraints, contractures, and 4 hours of dialysis to sit thru...........and YOU got a SMILE this morning as BIG as the SUN! You are truly God's message to us all. So Facebook what we complaining about today?? Really?? Aww....ok...

Philippians 4:11 NKJV "Not that I speak in regard to need, for I have learned in whatever state I am, to be content"

The Lord gave me these words to share with someone during the journey: **Sometimes you have to smile even though you want to cry, but rest assured, at some point, your heart will catch up with your smile.**

Chapter 13
God Kept Me

"Thou wilt keep him in perfect peace, whose mind is stayed on thee: because he trusteth in thee." Isaiah 26:3

I was exhausted, angry, disappointed, frustrated, and at one point, hopeless. This was my real life, and it was hard. It was by no means easy, but it was doable in God's strength. The constant leading and confirmation from God's word kept me. Many people have asked me over time, what is it that keeps you going. It's hard for me to answer that question with just one thing. At different times during our journey, something different kept me pushing through to the next. I've tried to think back and list them now in retrospect.

The desire to do God's will, kept me. The people around me that could see God in our situation and were blessed by our journey kept me. The knowledge of God's presence kept me. Knowing that this is bigger than me kept me.

The expectation of something great taking place kept me. The love for my son kept me. The love for my family kept me. The desire for Corion's experience to be a positive one for Jacori kept me. The love I witnessed between Corion and his nephew, Jace, kept me. The love I experienced from my husband and his family kept me. The love the caregivers had for him kept me.

I was surrounded by God's presence even though I didn't realize it fully at the time. Constantly seeing miracles kept me going. The challenge of it all kept me going. I've always liked being challenged and this was a doozy. Corion's strength kept me going. I always told him he was the strongest man I know.

The fact that Corion said that he was not in pain kept me. The fact that he still had his sense of humor during so many difficult moments and issues, kept me and even made me ashamed to complain. The fact that he kept waking up from one day to the next kept me.

When he asked me *"Do you believe me, Ma? I just want you to believe me,"* kept me going. When he told me to *"write everything down, we gone change the world"* kept me going. The many people that came to me and said how this journey had blessed them, kept me going. The fact that he is my firstborn and only son, kept me going.

Our testimony kept me going. The ultimate miracle of his living kept me going. His smile kept me going. His laughter kept me going. His encouragement kept me going. His peace kept me going. His love and admiration kept me going.

God's Holy Spirit kept me going. The promises of God kept me going. And now, even though sometimes I may appear to be alone, I am never really alone because the presence of God and the love of my dear sweet son dwells inside like an unyielding spring of life.

The unconditional love, acceptance, peace, understanding and divine protection I've longed for all my life are now within me. I've come to learn internal needs cannot be obtained from an external source, but only from the kingdom of God.

12/11/2014 (social media post)

God surely knows what you need. Sometimes life these days for me can become completely overwhelming but I pray and ask God to help me, help my family, and to continue to give us the strength to do the work He has laid before us. It is my belief that if He brings you to it, He will certainly bring you through it. Yesterday I heard from God in many ways in answer to my prayer for help to keep going. But the most encouraging was the excitement in Corion's face last night when I made it to see him. I had seen him earlier briefly in dialysis and I usually don't see him again on Wed, but I've been off my routine for the past week and needed to spend some time with him. When I entered the room he said, "You are the best person. You get me everything I need bruh. You take care of your kids, you just something else, for real. You the best momma in the world mane. I almost want to cry. I love you mane for real, I do. You the best momma in the world." I ain't trying to be the best momma in the world, I just try to do whatever it is God has blessed me to be able to do in hopes that my children and my husband feel loved and appreciated in this world. I love being a mother and a wife. As hard as this year has been for me and my family, it has truly been a blessing. If you've ever gone through an extraordinary difficulty in your life, you'll understand what I mean. Sometimes your struggle is your greatest blessing. We are truly blessed. Have an awesome day Faces and be the best at whatever it is God has laid before you.

God has given me dreams that have manifested. He has led and directed me throughout this journey. He has been with me all my life actually; I just didn't recognize nor acknowledge His presence.

The Bible is our guide for life. When we read it through a natural lens, it may be hard to understand. I read the scriptures now and they give me a view and meaning to my life. I must read the word daily. It's God's love letter to those who choose to believe. I will admit that sometimes the dreams and the experiences were and continue to be scary. But the word of God says that God has not given us the spirit of fear. I also know His word says that He will never leave me nor forsake me.

My Village

Being a caregiver is a difficult job. Much like that of a mother, but harder. Being the eyes, ears, understanding and decision-maker for an adult is an even more daunting job, to say the least. I always tried to show my appreciation for the support and care from the medical staff. A few years into the journey, someone said something to me that lifted a huge burden off me mentally. They encouraged me to consider the nursing facility an extension of my home.

Sometimes we can beat ourselves up, feel ashamed and give in to the pressures of what others think, even when we are doing our best. I began to call where he lived "his room" as if it was a room in my home. I stopped feeling bad that I was unable to care for him where I slept. I also stopped allowing what others thought make me feel ashamed.

It was never my thought that nursing home care would be a long-term circumstance. I surely hoped that he would get back on his feet enough for in-home care. But that wasn't the case for me. I looked into it many times, but I couldn't care for him full-time and work. I needed their help, and I truly appreciated everyone that provided care. The love a few showed was the icing on the cake.

I considered my incredible support system my village. We've encountered many on this journey, but the village was those that seemed to always be there without fail. They were key to my survival through this season. God placed all the right people in the right places. My husband was my greatest support and place to break down when it all became too much for me to bear. I loved that he took the initiative to ensure we got time away to regenerate and build a strong bond as a couple. We needed this strength to continue the journey as one.

My daughter and grandchildren kept me grounded in the reality of life. They gave me a constant reason to keep going, as not only did Corion need me, but they needed me as well. Corion especially enjoyed the laughter and joy they would bring. We never needed a crowd when we all came together for birthdays, holidays, and family time.

My sisters, Crystal and Ericka, were my sounding board, source of humor, and reassurance. Crystal was always there, traveling from Chicago to Memphis at the drop of a dime. She wanted to be fully present with every aspect of the journey for her "brother". And I would be remiss not to mention how her friends were always supportive. They stepped in for her many times when she couldn't be there. I am so thankful for her friends.

My cousin Tiffany was the number one cookie fairy. She would send care packages and cards so often. He was never low on supply. I had to ask her to stop at one time because I was running out of places to stash cookies and treats. Her consistent love and attention meant so much to us both.

My in-laws were always amazing. They all quickly adapted to Corion's behavior issues and kept the humor and family time coming. Chris would check on Corion and go by our house to feed our dog, Carter, whenever we traveled. As both my beautician and sister-in-love, LaKitta kept my hair looking good so that I never had to wear my pain on the outside. She also made sure all of us were always fed both physically and spiritually. She would visit with Corion without any prompting, just to make sure we were straight. She and Dre had a ramp added to their home so that he could visit comfortably. That, for me, is truly loved beyond measure.

My inner circle, Timikka, Nancy, Michele, and Jennifer, listened to me cry, scream, give up, get back up and keep going. They would be a great sounding board and source of encouragement. Anytime we had a big moment, I could count on them all to take out the time to come to join in on the celebration or even the difficult moments.

My Bestie, Timikka, doesn't live in Memphis, but she was here for every occasion. She would even bring Corion's dad along for the ride. I am especially thankful for the times she encouraged me to continue to make the posts on Facebook. She told me it was helping many people more than I knew, and she knew that it was encouraging for me as well. I appreciate her so much!

Timikka (post comment) 10/15/2016
God is always with you and so are all your friends and family…no matter how many times you feel like you're falling we are here to lift you up. You seem so strong, and you don't have to be all the time. Crying is part of the healing process. I love you, Sis always.

My employer was always patient and flexible with my time. Many of my co-workers became more like family. Donna would always send care packages to Corion. She is such a sweet lady. He made a video for her once to tell her how much he appreciated her. Nancy was also amazing support. She was at the facility so much they assumed she was another one of Corion's many aunts, as she truly is in spirit. I can't really recall a moment when she wasn't there for me. We are blessed to have such an angel here on earth.

My church family supplied prayers and spiritual strength. They were the foundation on which I stood and reached back for in times of weakness. I am especially thankful for the consistent visits from my Pastor Sylvester Hamilton and Minister Willie Dodson & his wife, Janie. They were always there even when I wasn't.

The Anoxic Brain Injury Caregivers Support Group I found on Facebook was such a Godsend for me. They understood the many challenging things that others could not begin to understand. I quickly realized no matter how bad things are in life, someone just may well be having a worse time than you. So, we must be thankful for all things, no matter how difficult the circumstance.

Corion's friends Arbeny, Jason, Jasmine L., and later, Derrick, were consistent. There were definitely others on occasion, but these are the ones I recall most. They would visit and provide the youthful energy he needed. Though he didn't want them to see him the way he was. He certainly appreciated the time spent over the years.

Though sometimes I may have felt alone, God made sure I was never truly alone. In hindsight, I can see that we had an amazing support system. I am eternally grateful to them all.

Chapter 14

The Spiritual Battle

"For we wrestle not against flesh and blood, but against principalities, against powers, against the rulers of the darkness of this world, against spiritual wickedness in high places."
Ephesians 6:12

DISCLAIMER
I would like to make this disclaimer. In no way am I making a claim nor intend to imply the experience that I am sharing is the case for any other individual other than my son. I highly respect the medical profession, and even more, the patients and their families that suffer with brain injury and other cognitive-related issues. I am only referencing my personal experience with my son and the journey we were on. I sought God for my answers. It is my personal faith and relationship with God that I rely on for my beliefs, views, opinions, and understanding regarding our specific circumstances.

Early in the journey, I recall a doctor's appointment, where the nurse asked Corion who I was to him. They talked to him to calm him as they attempted to put him under anesthesia before a procedure. He said to the nurse in a loving, sweet voice, *"my wonderful mother."* But another time, when someone asked him the same question, the answer came out as *"the mother"* or *"the momma."* For a long time, he told me I was not his mother. Most times, he called everyone that took care of him, mother. Corion generally calls me *"Ma,"* but I soon noticed a different tone to his voice when he vehemently says, "Mother" and also uses extremely profane language. This was not our experience before his injury.

When he would go into a rage and attack me, I couldn't understand why. I felt like he hated me, and I was doing all I could to show him love. I wonder if that is how God feels? Does He consistently love us, and we reject Him, curse Him, and tell Him about all the things He isn't doing for us? Interesting thought, huh.

I must acknowledge here that brain-injured patients are often left with behavioral issues similar to those Corion exhibited. The Rancho Levels chart is used to characterize awareness, cognition, and behavior levels after brain injury. I had done my research and tried to become familiar with aspects of anoxic brain injury. I could see where my son's behavior compared to the chart.

Even though it was expected that he would act out somehow, for me, there was something different about his behavior. He would be sweet and kind with me, but other times he would fly into a rage without anything I could point to as a trigger. I tried to dismiss it as a symptom of his brain injury. But our deeper conversations, my encounter with the prophet, my own personal experiences and my motherly instinct let me know it was definitely something more to our particular situation.

He's Searching for You

So, during the last week in August of 2016, Corion had been having a very difficult time in dialysis each day. On Thursday of that week, I went by the facility to ensure his cable was paid, and that money was in his trust. I generally would visit Corion after work, but this day, I felt a strong need to go to the nursing facility in the middle of the day.

When I got there, the lady at the front desk did something she never did before, nor again after this time. She got on the intercom to announce, "Visitor for Corion Reed." I thought that was strange. I actually felt like they were hiding something, and they had to warn them that I was headed that way. Nursing care isn't an option I would choose after this experience; however, we had to make the best of it at that time. I am glad I could be there for my son because many residents didn't have family to help care for them. Family support is vital in this setting.

When I got to his room, the Unit Manager, beckoned for me to come into the room directly across from him. Two ladies resided in this room, Ms. Payne and Ms. Austin. Ms. Payne had asked to speak with me. Apparently, her and the nurse had been having a discussion about me. When I walked in, she said, "We've been waiting for you."

What? They didn't know I was coming. The Unit Manager went on to say that Ms. Payne was a prophetess and she had something she wanted to share with me. I agreed to listen, but I wasn't able to look at her for some reason. It's as if I had been taken up into a spiritual realm.

The light was so bright in the room, that I could not open my eyes and I immediately began to shed tears. I can't remember her exact words, but I know she told me that Corion calls for me in the night. She said he was searching for me. She said that she answered him one night he was calling, "*Momma come here*", but when she did, he told her, "*You not my momma.*"

76

She says that he had unclean spirits in him. She asked me did I understand, and I told her that I did. She said that the spirits are after me, and not him. She told me that I had something I had to do for the Lord. She again asked me if I understood. We could hear the spirit talking and trying to distract us as she was speaking to me. She said, "Do you hear him?" I replied, "Yes ma'am I do."

Then suddenly the blinding bright light went out, I opened my eyes and thanked her. While I'm writing, I can also recall that she enjoyed oatmeal cookies. I purchased some at one time as a token of appreciation. They told me that they had tried to pray the spirits away but were unsuccessful. It was me that the spirits wanted. I actually didn't understand then, the way I understand it now.

Territory and Authority

In 2020, I learned while listening to Stephanie Ike, that spirits have authority over territories. You have to have a place of authority over a territory to come against an unclean spirit. The Lord gives us authority over territory He sends us into. The ladies had faith, but they did not have the authority over the territory in which the spirits ruled. I apparently had some level of authority, but I didn't understand my position at the time. God has placed everything we need for this life inside of us. But we may not know how to activate or access the ability and authority we possess.

After this spiritual encounter with the ladies, I went into Corion's room. I sat on his bed just so in awe and fear. Then Corion said to me *"it's deep ain't it*". I agreed and told him, "It's too deep for me." I did not feel equipped nor capable for whatever it was God wanted me to do.

I thought, Lord, what have I gotten myself into. He even told me once during this same time, *"It's easy Ma"*. Nothing seemed easy to me. But many times, we are being in the natural, over complicate things of the spirit. The word says His yoke is easy and His burdens are light. In our natural sense, we are unable to discern things of the spirit.

1 Corinthians 2:14 "But the natural man receiveth not the things of the Spirit of God: for they are foolishness unto him: neither can he know them, because they are spiritually discerned."

God Sees Me!

About one month after the prophecy, I went to visit Corion on a Saturday morning. He seemed to be angrier with me than usual. He scolded me saying, *"You ain't doing NOTHING! You ain't been going to church. You been cussing! You ain't doing nothing."* My first thought was, Wow! Then I thought, "Oh my God! How did he know that? How was he aware that I had decided to not go any further in my faith?" I had started to doubt God's presence, and second guess His voice. I tried to convince myself that all I had experienced up to this point wasn't really a miracle. Maybe it was just all in my head. The devil was even trying to convince me that I was going crazy.

But then I also realized within myself, if he can see me, then God can see me. It was like a revelation. You know we've heard this for years, and we believe it to be true. But now I KNOW THIS, know this! There was no doubt. How else could this man know what I am doing when he isn't with me. I quickly did whatever I had come to do for him and went home, but I was sooo nervous. I didn't know what to do. I tried to sleep and couldn't. I tossed and turned all night.

So, I got up early the next morning, went into my secret place and repented. I pleaded with God to please forgive me and that I would do His will. I knew that we were in the midst of a miracle, and I had allowed my emotions and disappointment to get the best of me. But God and Corion knew there was a purpose to be fulfilled, even if I didn't understand it. I had to honor my position and get back in the fight.

His Grace is Sufficient

God will always use something you already have. Your blessing is going to come from something already inside of you. God will always work with the container and contents. So, without much direction, armed with the bible and my faith, I went to see Corion the next day. He greeted me and I sat in a chair beside his bed which was extremely low to the floor to prevent a fall. I opened my bible and began to read a scripture. I'm not certain which, but I'm sure it was inspired by the Holy Spirit because it definitely caused a response.

As I read, Corion spewed so much blasphemy and expletives it was unbelievable. When Corion is speaking, you can hardly understand what he is trying to say. But when this spirit speaks, he is clear, precise and very direct. The spirit said God wasn't real and seemed to be mocking Jesus. I'm certain he called me many derogatory names as well. But I stayed calm and continued to read as I thought I should. He even reached for me and scratched me at that moment.

After some time, he began to speak to an invisible group that was apparently cowering away. He said, "Y'all leaving. Y'all just gone leave like that. Y'all some punks mane. Bye. Bye. Bye." He then stopped speaking but he couldn't make eye contact with me. His eyes were really shifty, and the Holy Spirit let me know, even though he seemed calm like it was over, a stronghold still existed.

Then, suddenly, in a calm voice, my son's true spirit, said, "I love you ma. I like when you bring him with you." There was no one physically with me, so I asked, "Who?" He replied, "God's friend." I wasn't sure what that meant of course, so I just nodded in agreement. It was Sunday and I needed to head to church, especially since I'd already been scolded the day before. LOL.

I was listening to gospel radio the next day. They always have a bible question of the day for the listeners. As I got into the car, heading to work, they were asking the question "Who is God's friend?" Wow again! I was so interested to hear this answer. The response was, Abraham (James 2:23). Abraham is God's friend. I was astonished. Was Abraham with me yesterday? This is how God began to speak with me and I've continued to listen.

Before I left him on Sunday, I told him that I would be back later. However, that day was exhausting, and I didn't make it back. So on my lunch break Monday, as normal, I went to see him in dialysis. His sitter, Candi, was surprised when I walked in the door. She said, he had been saying all morning, "She said she was coming back. She said she was coming back." Then Candi said before I walked through the door, he told her, "*Here she come now.*" Once again, he confirmed that he could see me without my being physically present. I was then sure we were dealing with something much bigger than ourselves.

I still had no idea of what to do, how to do it, or what the plan was. I had always been a person that lived my life by lists and plans. This situation was one that was totally out of my control and required me to trust the process. I had to throw my full faith and hope in God's plan, whatever it was. But I knew, if He trusted me with it, then He prepared me for it.

I could no longer deny that we were in a spiritual battle. This was probably when I began to be more personal with the Lord. When we came upon a challenge, I found myself saying, "Lord, I can't *WAIT* to see how you fix this!" I would ask that He make the crooked paths straight. I knew I needed some of God's strength to carry me through each day.

I slowly became aware and unashamed of my limitations. For I know, where I run out, God is always there to bring His will to pass. He armed me with faith, patience, persistence, and most of all LOVE!

09/16/2016 (social media post)
Truly enjoyed service on today. The devil tried to stop us, but I've told
him "I wasn't built to give up!" I am so thankful to my loving and
understanding church family. We are in the midst of a miracle, and I
am ever so grateful to all that join me in praying God's will be done.
Don't be distracted by what you see, but remember it, so you can help
us tell the story of our God's goodness and glory in time. On the way

home Corion said "I'm proud of you Mama. I'm so happy you are my Mama." God's grace is sufficient. He is raising up an army.

---

2 Corinthians 12:9 And he said unto me, My grace is sufficient for thee: for my strength is made perfect in weakness. Most gladly therefore will I rather glory in my infirmities, that the power of Christ may rest upon me.

Chapter 15
Testing the Spirits

"Dear friends, do not believe every spirit, but test the spirits to see whether they are from God, because many false prophets have gone out into the world." 1 John 4:1

One sunny June afternoon in 2020, Jacori, Corion and I sat outside to try and get some sun. I also thought it would be good for them to spend some needed father and son time throwing the ball. Well, it was more like torture than what I had in mind. I could not get Corion to cooperate. He was so angry and aggressive.

I was finally frustrated with trying and attempted to take him inside, but he was in a fighting mood. When this happens, I generally leave him for a while. Today this spirit wasn't passing quickly. Jacori came over and said, "Let me try Gigi." Corion calmed down enough for us to get him back into the house and to his bedroom.

Just after I got him settled in his room, Jacori asked, "What does 'I rebuke you' mean?" I was puzzled by his question, but I explained it was normally said to make the devil flee. He replied, "I said it to myself outside." Wow!! The definition in google states, to speak severely to them because they have said or done something that you do not approve of. There are several times in scripture where it says, Jesus rebuked the unclean spirits. The same way Corion loved his "Grannyma", Jacori loves his Gigi. Boys are natural born protectors.

Journal Entry 06/18/20

In prayer this morning, I read 1 John 4. My topic was light in darkness. I am looking for God to change the atmosphere in my home back to love, peace, joy, and understanding and I pray that He does the same in the world. The spirit of God must be a light in this dark place. We must shine so that people have hope. The Antichrists are here, says John. We must be the reminder that God is still in control. I've had some difficult moments with Corion, but for Jacori to pray in himself "I rebuke you" and give some relief for me shows that God is still in control. Hallelujah!! Thank you Jesus!

I had prayed with Jacori more than a week before as prompted by God. I shared with him that he is special and won't be like other kids because of the things he's seen and experienced concerning his father. I assured him that he is fine just the way he is and admonished him to follow God. I told him that he will have many choices to make in life, but if he chooses those that glorify God, everything will work out even when it is difficult. I am so glad that I prayed with him as I was led to because he was surely a great help to me, especially in this moment. This moment also reminded me when we allow God to lead us, things will be "easy" just as Corion told me it would be.

Do you know who I am?

There were many times Corion, and I had this battle with competing spirits. I recall a moment during the early days of our journey, we were sitting in the courtyard of the first rehab. I was trying to get Corion to catch a small ball. He was just shaking his head at me, refusing to cooperate. Jace's dad, Jordan, was visiting at the time. Corion looked at him and said, *"Why won't she just give up man?"* I told him, "Cause I'm not a quitter." I had no idea then that the fight had just begun.

When I visited with Corion one night at the next facility, he cursed at me and was extremely mean towards me for the first time. It was quite shocking. Staring into his eyes, I said, "I don't know who you are, but you are not my son. My son would never speak to me in that way." The spirit did flee but only for a while.

Over time, the occurrences became more and more frequent. One night after he came home, I had decided just to sit still. I listened to him spew all types of cusswords towards me. Then he said, *"Cry or something!"* Just as I did when I was that stubborn child getting a whipping with no tears, I refused to cry today. Then he said, *"Leave like you always do."* He was right. In hindsight, this was my way of avoiding confrontation out of fear. I usually walked away or left the nursing facility when he behaved this way. I didn't want to deal with him when he was like this. But at home, in this time, I was forced to face my fears.

Besides, apparently leaving didn't make the situation better. I can now see that it made the spirit stronger, or as he said, *"grown now."* Before I could learn to recognize the difference between the unclean spirit and Corion, I first had to acknowledge that there was one. After that it was easy to recognize the spirit when he would be vulgar and extremely aggressive. When Corion wanted to get his point across he would be aggressive, but differently somehow.

I knew my son's spirit, because I've known him all of his life, but it was hard in the beginning to know when his true spirit was speaking. His true spirit would speak quickly and in a code like manner. He would say, *"Do you see me ma?" "Do you know me?" "I don't cuss at all."* Whereas the unclean spirit would be clear, direct and matter of fact. He would also ask, *"Do you know who I am?"*

The greatest difference is that most conversations with the unclean spirit included lies. They were not just any lie, but the same lies he's told me about myself most of my life. The enemy is cunning that way. He will speak to things that you are already insecure about. Evil spirits are drawn to how we think, and we can be oppressed by them because of this.

One day, just like many times before, Corion asked me *"Do you know who I am now?"* This time I said, "You look like Corion & your voice is like him. Who are you?" He said, *"That's who I am, Corion Reed."* I then went on to ask, "What's your whole name?" I got no answer.

Then he said, *"Corion Black."* I just responded in a dismissive tone, "Aw ok", to signal to that spirit that I know you are not my son. Then Corion, my son's true spirit, stepped forward with great authority and said *"Corion D'Shawn Reed Black"*.

I asked, "Who am I?" Then the spirit confidently said, *"Crystal Reed"*. Again, I ignored the spirit (resist & he shall flee) and with more strength, Corion said, *"Chondrea Denise Reed Black!"* Then, as always, I asked, "I am your?" and his response *"my mother."* I said, ok there you are. He said, *"How you get up here?"*

Sometimes I would ask him, "Where is Corion?" and he would say, *"Corion is gone forever"*. At one point during this period, I decided to call my son Bubba. The response I received was him taken aback. "Bubba" he laughed. I kept it up. I began to consistently refer to my son as "Bubba", as it seemed to have confused the enemy. Corion and I developed our own way of communicating, so that he knew that I had caught on. I refused to allow the enemy to outsmart me in everything. I had learned to use wisdom and spiritual discernment.

As I began to grow in my knowledge of the word, the spirit began to tell me, *"You know me well"*. He even said once, *"You know me too well."* I asked Corion one morning while I was engaging with the spirit, "How many are there?" And he quickly answered, *"Ten"*. Then the spirit said to me, *"You tricky Mother."* Since I didn't know how to get rid of him, I figured I needed to learn something from him. God will use your enemies to bring you in line with His word.

I learned to change the atmosphere in the room through worship music and that worked for a while. Then I learned to arrest the spirit before entering the room by praying for myself and asking the Holy Spirit to go before me and stand with me.

This was powerful; prayer works! I believe it was comforting for Corion too, because I distinctly remember coming into his room to watch a program with him and he said so lovingly, *"It's me time."* We enjoyed so many moments together, in spite of the battle we were up against.

The spirit soon began to acknowledge that I knew who he was, but I soon realized it wasn't so much about me knowing who he was. It was more about me knowing WHO I AM in Christ!!! Once I began to learn of the power I possessed through Christ, that spirit had to go and a stronger one replaced him.

An unclean spirit is covert and likes to hide to not be seen for who it is. But Christ is the truth and the light. When you shine the light on the enemy through the truth of God's word, the enemy must flee. Lies can no longer hold you once the truth has been made known. The truth sets you free.

His True Spirit

Corion had a true warrior spirit. He was a born fighter! He has always been a fighter naturally, but now God was teaching Him to be a fighter spiritually. Even when he wanted to give up, he came back stronger. He got that from his mother. This fighting spirit is how he lasted 6 years through so much adversity. But there comes a time when even the greatest fighter is tired and no longer wants to fight.

When he came home from the hospital in 2018, in a video I asked, "What do you need?" He replied, "*Some time and some help.*" I had to learn to put on the whole armor of God so that I could help him fight the good fight. He told me I was on his team.

In July 2020, I wrote in my journal when Corion said to me, "*I'm proud of you ma. You took all my cards.*" This was after us listening to yet another sermon by Jakes. God gave me a prayer to teach him, to use when he felt agitated. I wanted him to say, Lord please take control of my mind. But He insisted on saying, "*Lord take control of my body.*" He would tell me, "*I am a child of God*", other times, he'd say, "*I am a man of God.*" As his flesh would weaken, his true spirit would grow stronger.

His true spirit always reverenced God. He would also encourage me to keep fighting. He even told both Robert and I one night that he was sorry for everything and loved us both. That was his true spirit; always loving, protective, caring, and respectful. Many times, he would insist, "*I don't curse at all.*" Again, that was his way of trying to teach us the differences. We just couldn't understand at the time. I do remember him warning me before he left, "*Don't cuss momma. Don't cuss.*" That was my vice before I found Christ.

I found an old journal of Corion's. He liked to write as well. In this journal he had written down top 5 dream jobs. They were 1. Sports broadcaster, 2. Basketball Coach, 3. Basketball Player, 4. Preacher, and 5. Lawyer. He could had definitely been successful at either.

It took me some time to realize when Corion spoke about hell he called it "*Mississippi.*" I have gone back and forth in my mind, and I can only conclude that he may have experienced a trauma as a child/teen in Mississippi that was hell for him. This may have been his interpretation, for him to have a point of reference. He would say it STINKS! He said to me "*You ran to me. You called me up here.*" And sometimes he sounded as if he was out of breath in saying "*I ran up here*" when Corion's true spirit was trying to tell me something quickly.

In recent months, I asked God, why did He use Corion. The Holy Spirit responded, "Because you would not have believed anyone else." God knows me so well. He will allow an irritant to provoke you to make a change in you that needs to happen. It will point out something you are already ashamed of, and pain plays an important role in the process.

Everyone doesn't get a second chance to right their wrongs. I am thankful to God that he allowed Corion and I to strengthen our bond. We were able to show appreciation for one another in this time. We got a better understanding of who we truly were created to be in this earth. It is my prayer that others can do this while they have breath in their body.

Chapter 16

It's For Others

"I have declared the former things from the beginning; and they went forth out of my mouth, and I shewed them; I did them suddenly, and they came to pass." Isaiah 48:3

Sometimes I cry and get upset because I miss my son so much. When I look at photos, especially when he was a child, I wonder why he couldn't just grow up, have a family, and still be alive getting on my nerves like other children are with their moms. I asked God, "why did you have to take my son?" And He answered me and said, "Because he wasn't yours; he was mine. And when you have finished, I will come and get you also." God only loans us these souls on earth for a little while, especially one as special as Corion.

We had such a beautiful year in 2017 with minimal time in the hospital. When Corion was in the hospital in 2018, he told me *"It's my time. I'm tired. My body has betrayed me. I am ready to go."* But I assumed he was speaking of going from the hospital to home. I talked to my husband on the phone and Corion overheard me telling him what he had told me. After I got off the phone, he said, *"I'm serious. It's my time."* As I was feeding him that night, he went on to say, *"I have a house waiting for me."* He tried to say something else, but he could not make it clear to me. It appeared that there was a spiritual force that would not allow

91

him to speak clearly as he had been. He would instead only say, "*Ha Ha Ha*".

I told my son I was okay. I felt as though I would be fine if he were to pass away, especially witnessing the many challenges he had to bear daily. But I guess the Lord knew I wasn't, and that his work on earth wasn't yet complete. Then, I assume the Holy Spirit must have spoken to him, because after some quiet time, he blurted out, "*It's not for us; it's for others.*"

After that encounter, I was able to make the connection to the time he was talking to Jace around 2016 when he said, "*I ain't gone leave you mane.*" It was in a tone of frustration for him, but reassurance for Jace. It's like he wanted to go, but he had something else more important to keep him here.

Sometimes, many times, life just doesn't seem fair. But we must remember that all things work together for the good to them called according to His purpose. And also, that God's thoughts are not our thoughts, and His ways are not our ways. I've learned that we must strive to endure every season that looks like hardship.

We do not know God's plans, but we can be assured that they are for a greater purpose that is bigger than us. I am happy to be a part of His plan for someone else's success in life. If our experience can help someone else gain a better understanding, and begin to accept God's plan for their life, then it was surely worth it all.

10/22/18 (Anoxic Group Post)

So Corion is in the hospital and has been for the past 5 days due to complications from a new medication. He had surgery to repair his dialysis access……. BUT….we had a conversation. He asked me to be strong. He said his body is tired and that he is ready to go. He says he has a "house" waiting for him. We talked about many things, and he even recalled himself in the past which he normally doesn't remember at all. I was telling my husband about our conversation on the phone and once I hung up he said I heard you talking. He said, I'm serious….it's my time. He doesn't know when, but he said he is ready, and I guess I need to be too. I am thankful to God for this conversation. And if it's soon or much much later, I am thankful for each moment , second, day and hour we spend together. He also told me that this isn't for us but it's for other people. That confirms what the Lord spoke to me after this happened Jan 2014. I needed to share this with someone. Thanks for listening. On my way to see my guy at the hospital because he yet lives. He is truly the strongest man I know.

Back in the Fight

After he returned to his room at the facility, we had a great conversation. He was in good spirits, and he was surely back in the fight. I made a video post on my social media account this particular night. The most significant thing I remember from this night was when he said to me, *"Let Him do his thang ma please! Let him do his thang!"*

When you are going through difficulty in life, it can often be hard to see God's hand at work. I always knew that this journey was bigger than us, because God told me so, and I believe Him. But looking back, it blows my mind. I heard it said best, this way, "You are more awake in retrospect, than you are when you are going through it."

Not Here for Himself

As I read through text messages between me and Keke, I am sure Corion stayed for us; not for himself. He came really close to death in 2018. After a long, difficult battle with an infection, he came back stronger. His words were clear, and his natural personality came thru stronger than ever before. *"I never expected something like this to happen to me. You never know what's gone happen."* He said it so calm and clear. There was so much strength in his voice after this.

I began to realize that he really did understand what was going on, and that he was trapped inside his head trying hard to come through. He would ask me often, *"Do you see me ma?"* or *"Do you know who I am?"* He would also ask, *"Do you believe me ma? I just want you to believe me."*

A text on 10/25/18, from Keke, my sister-in-love, confirmed what I suspected. She said in her text:

> *Corion is in there listening to the things you say. He says it's like it's a demon that he's fighting against. He also gets frustrated because of his condition. It's a spiritual war that you are fighting. The attacks are against you. Why, because it was your faith in God that caused him to still be here. Even in God, he never said the road would be easy. Trust the process. Many times you have given up. But God gives you a word thru Corion to let you know it's not in vain. It's ok to walk away. But walking away doesn't mean you're defeated. Just get you a lil break, go back and fight a lil more. You have come so far, many times Alone. It's really hard to explain but I know you understand me. I don't know*

God's plan, but the Enemy knows your strength when you're at your best.

I was so happy that someone else could see what I could see. I didn't want to continue to fight this spiritual battle alone and God certainly knew it. Her statement that the attacks were against me confirmed what the lady in the room across from him had told me a few years earlier. By now I had heard this more than once, so it was no surprise, but still hard to fully accept. It was comforting that someone close to me could understand what I was dealing with and that I wasn't losing my mind.

After I responded that I understood her text and that it was actually confirmation for me, she texted me this message:

> *In the name of Jesus, the devil has got to flee. He may never be fully recovered, but I truly believe that we pray, believe and have faith God will shift the atmosphere so it won't be so hard on you. Get a prayer cloth, oil etc. And just cover him. Demons can't live under all that. They gotta flee. It's a spiritual war. And we gotta put our big girl panties on and fight back cause satan is not going to win!!*

Just before her text, I had already prayed, "Lord I'm back in the ring. Devil I'm declaring war. It's time for you to go cause I've seen Corion last night and many times before and in his words, he says, *'I'm fine'*."

The night we were texting, Corion was really talkative. He went on to say, *"We doing good. We almost there. It's getting better and better. He making it better suddenly!"* He even asked, *"Why all these folks doing stuff for me like I'm a lil person?"* That night on my way home from the nursing home, I was so in awe and happy that I could have run beside the car rather than drive it.

Back in the Hospital

We'd taken a three-day trip to Atlanta with Corion in tow. My sister came along to help us, as well we had Jacori. They got to visit with Cory and his family. The trip was supposed to have been for my 30th year class reunion but it turned out to be more of a mission trip for Corion. It turned out to be an amazing trip.

In September, Robert and I celebrated our 25th wedding anniversary with family and friends. As usual, Corion stole the show. I told you he was always the life of the party. This time turned out to be no different. When he saw me that night, he said, "*You look gorgeous Ma.*" I said, "Boy don't make me mess up my makeup." He had an incredible time, and was even able to remember some of the event days later.

But October thru December was mostly spent in and out of the hospital. After doing well for a while in October, we had to spend Thanksgiving there. It was truly an emotionally draining time, and I didn't really want to go on, let alone watch him go through so much. I was trying to be strong, but I had also learned that I didn't have to be strong by the world's terms. God had been building my ability to lean in and not try to control the outcome of life's circumstances totally. I was learning the things I could change and the things that were beyond my control. Those things were God's business and not for Chon to take on. Cause He surely knew that I would try.

There were complications with his catheter access, and one had to be placed in his groin. That was not good and expected to be a last resort effort to continue dialysis. The doctors cautioned that he would most likely develop an infection quickly while using this area. Not to mention he was diapered so that would also make it difficult. Corion had a history of pulling his catheter out, so there was nothing positive about this option per our history.

I had been thru a few emotions, but true to form, I quickly moved into survival mode. My search was on for a few items I felt would help mitigate infection risk. The catheter covers that the hospital used were really expensive in their form, but I am persistent. I was able to purchase a comparable option thru an online medical supply company. The covers I found had a built-in chemical called Chlorhexidine gluconate (CHG) that I learned about in the hospital, which helps to prevent infections. They were more affordable than the hospital grade and helped to control his infections for nearly two years. I was surprised none of the medical professionals around us knew about them. BUT God!

My husband suggested that we purchase the tear-away basketball pants for better access to the catheter in the dialysis center. They served as the perfect solution to maintain his dignity during treatment. It is always important to consider a patient's dignity, especially when they have to depend totally on others for care.

We were back in the fight once again. My friend Michele would often tell me that I was built "Ford tough." I had to be, cause my guy was counting on me. During that November hospital stint, a commercial came on where the lawyer said, "We fight." Corion woke up and said, "*We fight, Mama.*" I answered with a tone of defeat, "We been fighting a minute!" He said, "*Fight some more!*" LOL! I guess he got me together real quick.

Hospital AGAIN

So, by December, he was discharged on a Thursday evening but rushed back Friday morning throwing up blood clots. Had 2 seizure like episodes in the ER, so they admitted him. Vomiting was from medication they gave to prevent clotting. His body just couldn't tolerate it. He got better and discharged within a couple of days.

I went to see Corion before work the day after his discharge because I was so worried about him. He was all smiles and laughter. This guy is so amazing! But even in the midst of that, he shared with me, "*I hate this; all of it!*" I quickly agreed and told him that I would pray God provides him some relief, whatever that looks like. He said, "*I love you ma and I know that God loves me.*"

We talked about a few more things and ended our conversation after warning me he was about to fart REAL loud. I told him to go for it! Ain't nobody like Corion. He surely made my day that morning. I shared this with my family and friends via text to make their day as well.

Though Corion expressed that he was ready to go, he lived almost two more years after this time. In 2020, he said to me, "*Took 2 years to find me. I'm grown now.*" He also said, "*I know where I am at. I know everything. I know more than you know.*" I now understand that he could see things that I could not see. I always wondered that, but now, I am assured of it.

07/27/2016 (social media post)
Sitting here with Corion Dshawn and you know what he said?
"You want to pray? Let's pray." And at the end of our prayer he
said "You want to run? Let's run." Then he asked for some
cookies. He been talking about prayer the last two weeks. It's
praying time fam! Let's pray!

Romans 12:12
Be joyful in hope, patient in affliction, faithful in prayer.

Chapter 17
He Has to Sing

"Sing praises to God and to his name! Sing loud praises to him who rides the clouds. His name is the Lord rejoice in his presence!" Psalm 68:4

Before his injury Corion enjoyed music and would sing on occasion. When he was about 5 years old, we were in the car and he said to me, *"I can sing but don't nobody know it"*. I said, "Really". Then he asked me, *"Why don't we ever go to church?"* I had no answer for the little guy. But if he wanted to go to church, then that was the new goal. We soon joined my husband's home church, Miracle Temple COGIC.

He sang in the choir at church and his school choirs in middle and high school. As he grew older, he began to shy away from singing for some reason. I assume it was due to peer pressure. But he had a beautiful melodic voice.

12/14/2018
So today Corion sang for one of his caregivers that didn't know he could sing. She cried. And she said she's not a crier. God is using him even in this bed! Let him use you!

Matthew 5:16
In the same way, let your light shine before others, so that they may see
your good works and give glory to your Father who is in heaven.

After his brain injury, I can recall one of our church sisters, Janie, asking him if he would sing again. She would always encourage him to sing, when she and her husband, Minister Willie Dodson, would visit him quite often.

Music became a great source of therapy for him. He enjoyed rap music, but when I put it on, he'd say, *"They did too much cussing, but I liked it though."* He could sing his favorite song from church, word for word, "Silver and Gold", by Kirk Franklin.

He also enjoyed, "God is Able", by Smokie Norful, and during the holiday season, "Let it Snow" by Boys to Men." Their Christmas album is an annual tradition in our home, so he knew the songs well. He told me once that his favorite song was "A Change is Gonna Come" by Sam Cooke. He's always had what the elders would call an old soul.

On our way home Christmas Eve 2015, he asked me, *"Do you talk to Him?"* Knowing he was referring to the Lord, I replied, "Yes". He then said, *"Did He tell you something?"* I said, "Yes". He responded, *"He said believe Him."* I don't know why I didn't make the connection then that he was truly having conversations with God.

But I've since learned that miracles happen in hindsight. We can't always see the manifestation of the miracle when it is occurring.

12/24/2015
Ain't nothin better than this boy sitting in this chair singing Boys to
Men Let it Snow! One day I'm going to record these conversations in
the car. He asked me do I talk to "Him"….did "He" tell you
something. "He said believe Him".

John 6:29
Jesus answered and said unto them, This is the work of God, that ye believe
on him whom he hath sent.

Singing in Darkness

In 2020, just before the quarantine began, Corion said to me *"I gotta sing"* more than once. Since I couldn't see him for a while, I made him a CD with a message, scriptures and worship music. On the CD, I told him to sing to the people in the facility and sing LOUD, from his bed of course. I thought it would be good for him and others.

He continued to express his need to sing after he came home to stay. He said he had to sing. We would turn on the music and sing. I also loved to play music to help his mood. It helped to change the atmosphere as well.

03/15/2020
Tonight he sang EVERY WORD of "Silver and Gold" He said he has
to sing

The command to sing is repeated more frequently than any command in the Bible, except the one to love. Music speaks to parts of the brain that words alone cannot. Music effects the spirit. Corion could remember things much better when I created a cadence or song.

Because the devil is the prince of the air, music can be used as a spiritual weapon to drive evil forces away. Just last week, I listened to a Bishop Jakes sermon called "Singing in the Dark". It speaks beautifully to our story. What resonates with me most is, the last time we were in the hospital, Corion said to me, *"I'm in darkness."*

In this message, Jakes explains how singing can affect the things we cannot control ourselves. Read that again! I am in constant awe of how God brings me a word that opens my understanding of so many things concerning our journey.

Knowing the effects of music, was my primary reason for the song selection at his homegoing service. The initial song, "When the Saints Go to Worship", by Benita Washington was played not only as an ode to our time together, but also to arrest the spirit in the room and usher in the presence of the Holy Spirit. It was my hope that others could experience the presence of God in the way that he and I had, especially during the last few months of his life.

I tried to find someone to sing it for me, but I couldn't. Then God spoke to me and said, "I told you to do it." I'm not much of a songstress, but I enjoyed having that final moment with Corion. And I could still hear him in the spirit encouraging me, just as he normally would. *"Sang Ma!"*

Isaiah 42:7
"To open eyes that are blind, to free captives from prison and to release from the dungeon those who sit in darkness."

Chapter 18
The Year 2020

"Behold, I will do a new thing; now it shall spring forth; shall ye not know it? I will even make a way in the wilderness, and rivers in the desert." Isaiah 43:19

In 2020, we all had to remain in our homes due to the worldwide pandemic. There was fear of the spread of the coronavirus, later referred to as COVID-19. During the pandemic, I've enjoyed listening to the sermons of Bishop TD Jakes, as well as several other online ministries.

I love how he shows us how the Old Testament relates to the New Testament. Then he "goes deeper" and brings that word to the present day! Oh, it excites me so much. In listening to him, I have been able to marry the early days of Corion's illness to the latter days in the same way. I am so grateful that my son told me in the beginning to *"write everything down. We gone change the world."*

Everything you Need is in the House

Corion said to me two years ago *"I have a house waiting for me."* When the quarantine began in March 2020, I heard in the spirit, "You have everything you need in the house." During this time at home, I've learned from my studies, the house is where God's presence is. He blew His breath into the body of man and gave Him life. He lives within us.

1 Corinthians 3:16
"Know ye not that ye are the temple of God, and that the Spirit of God dwelleth in you?"

We often overlook His presence by looking outside of ourselves to fill voids we have in our life. While we are busy trying to add to ourselves, our lives are best governed by subtraction, but we are so afraid to let go. When things are taken away, we can be free to honor God and operate in His power and not our own.

There was so much fear and uncertainty in this time. We had to quickly learn to let go of our normal way of doing things for a new way. While the world was working to coin the term, "new normal", I preferred to say that God is doing a new thing. I didn't like that term "new normal" much. There was nothing normal about it all for me.

I myself, much like others, was overwhelmed by fear. Corion was considered one of those who was part of the vulnerable population due to pre-existing conditions and living in a nursing facility. I was so worried without my watchful eye, that he would not be well taken care of, as I could not see him as I normally would.

But God spoke to me one day when I was overwhelmed. The Father asked me, "Do you think that you can take care of him better than I can?" That would be a "NO" for me, Sir. I apologized for "getting in His business" and calmed myself down. It also helped that my husband told me to stop watching the television. At the time, it seemed to be the greatest source of fear and uncertainty.

As I had feared, Corion did become ill during this time, but it was not due to the virus. I can recall when I woke up that morning, the spirit instructed me to "Be at peace today." I received a phone call from the nursing facility around noon. The nurse expressed that they were sending him to the hospital because he didn't look well. Dread and doom tried to grip me, but I remember the Holy Spirit's prompting and remained calm.

Because of the pandemic, we were told family was unable to accompany their loved ones in the hospital. BUT God! Since Corion could not speak for himself, he was part of a group of individuals who fell into an exception category, so I could accompany him. Did I tell you we were "exceptional"?! I considered this God's FAVOR!

Once they admitted him for severe dehydration, I was able to stay with him overnight, but I could not leave the room. My husband had to bring me clothes and food but leave it downstairs for a floor nurse to retrieve and bring it up to me. I wasn't concerned about the inconvenience, as long as I could stay with my son.

So many people were not making it out of the hospital, they were short staffed, and it was truly a scary time. But I wasn't afraid. I could hear the voice of the Lord comforting me and I knew that He was with us. Before discharge, God spoke to me once more regarding Corion saying, "He needs you now." I knew it was time for him to come home to stay under my care, especially until this virus was under control.

The insurance care coordinator quickly got to work to have him discharged to our home. She was so surprised that everything worked out within 24 hours. She told me more than once that they had never had a patient discharged from a nursing home to home within 24 hours. I assured her that this was God's plan. She agreed.

Even better, I was now working from home during this unusual time. The care coordinator helped us get setup with home health services and I could be there to supervise the care he received. I'd always wanted to be able to care for him from home, but it would have been difficult long term while I worked. This time was special and truly a blessing from God.

The miracle of it all for me is that even though he was a part of the vulnerable population, he was never affected by the virus. He continued to go to dialysis treatments as scheduled. With the virus so prevalent, there was a scare once with a person that had been in contact with his caregiver, but she tested negative for the virus. They were both fine and never experienced any of the symptoms.

Once we came home from the hospital, we found we had everything we needed in the house, just as the Holy Spirit had spoken to me at the beginning. I had been purchasing things over the years in anticipation of him coming home one day. Keke even surprised me with a delivery of supplies and his favorite snacks.

The house was representative of my natural house and my body (spiritual house) as a vessel where the Holy Spirit dwells. The time spent over the years working with the doctors, nurses and CNAs had groomed me for this task. I knew I would have to do most of it alone, but I knew how to change, feed, bath and administer his medication. I already had this knowledge within me.

I later learned that this spiritual *"house"*, was the same house Corion referred to when he was in the hospital two years earlier. I honestly believe he always knew his fate, especially since he would tell me often, *"I know more than you know."* He was kind of adamant about it now that I think back on it. When he got home to his room, he said with a sigh of relief, "This my room?" I was able to get him setup in the same bedroom he grew up in. I was happy to respond, "Yes baby, this is your room."

His sitter, Ms. Pat asked him during one of his dialysis treatments, "Corion, when you going back to the nursing home?" He told her without hesitation, *"I ain't NEVER going back there."* That hadn't been decided yet, but apparently, he knew, and he had decided for himself. He was right.

Being home wasn't so bad. We tried to get settled in a routine and enjoy the moment. We prayed against any negative spirits or sickness that may attempt to enter our house. We ate dinner and enjoyed each other's company as much as we could. My prayers had been answered, even with so much uncertainty looming. I often still tell others today that God shut the world down for me to spend the last few days, weeks, and months of life with our son at home. FAVOR once again. **To God be the Glory!**

Chapter 19
Everything Was Necessary

"So then, Christian brothers, because of all this, be strong. Do not allow anyone to change your mind. Always do your work well for the Lord. You know that whatever you do for Him will not be wasted" 1 Corinthians 15:58 (NLV)

I remember my sister, Crystal, saying that Corion wouldn't talk to anyone but me. He would say some things to others, but most times when people came around, he wouldn't speak to them as clearly and succinctly as he would to me, especially in the beginning. This got better over time, but I guess there are still many moments that were only meant for us to share.

Corion had a doctor's appointment on a Saturday his first week home. After the appointment, we decided to sit outside our house to enjoy some fresh spring air. With a reassuring tone, he said, *"Everything was necessary. It was all necessary."* I can now recall his tone as if he had been reflecting back on the past few years.

I genuinely believe he and God knew I would need those words and would come to depend on them after his departure. The Lord used him to encourage me in so many ways. I can also see how he used him for so many others that cared for him. God is so amazing.

Guilt, second guessing and the unfruitful thoughts of what I should have done, or could have done, was sometimes paralyzing because we had to rely solely on God's leading. There were no guarantees, and we didn't have much guidance from others. I've always been one to try to control the outcome of my circumstances, always striving for perfection in many areas of my life. I've come to learn that it's just not realistic.

I doubted the decision early on of allowing him to stay on the ventilator, thinking maybe we should have just agreed with the doctors back then and took him off. I remember sharing this thought with one of his good friends, Brandon. Corion called him "Big B". He quickly brought me back to reality with his response. He said, "How do you know that he would not have still lived?" This reminded me that our lives are in God's hand and that this was a God moment!! It's ALWAYS been a God moment.

Terrance, one of my sister's friends, told me while we were still in the throes of the initial event, "Chon, sometimes you just have to let everything break." I really appreciate those words. At the moment, I felt like I was trying to hold all the balls in the air of my life, and the weight was just too much to bear.

So, I put everything I thought I was controlling, in the hands of God. That was where I allowed the break to occur. It's like my life was shattered and all of the pieces were on the floor. Putting the pieces back together was next to impossible. But little by little God took each piece and placed it where He desired it to be. My then shattered mess is now a beautiful picture to me.

It's my prayer that our journey will help someone else facing similar circumstances. My life isn't perfect, but I love it. My family isn't perfect, but I love them unconditionally.

I genuinely believe that is how God's love is for us, His children. He loves us unconditionally. If we would only trust Him with EVERYTHING, He will place all things in His perfect will, and life would be beautiful…. not perfect…..but beautiful.

God doesn't waste anything concerning His children. I've learned that my blessings are connected to someone else's life and journey. There is a purpose and a plan for everything we go through in life. We may not understand it, but if we look unto Jesus, the author and finisher of our faith, we will see that his plans always worked together for our good.

I asked God in the beginning, "why Lord, why are you doing this". His response was that it was for the young people because many do not believe He is real. Then years later in 2018, I had a conversation with Corion while he was in the hospital. He told me clearly, *"It's for others"*. That was confirmation for me.

Just knowing he touched so many, and how much they loved him, warms my heart. It was so hard leaving him every day and wondering if I was doing the right thing, or if I should have quit working to care for him fulltime. That was really the hardest part for me mentally. I would cry in the car on my way home after each visit.

I wish I didn't have to care for him in a nursing home. It was especially difficult when others would ask, "When are you going to take him home?" But I had an idea of what I would be facing at home without the consistent support. It was a relief when God would show me how He had surrounded him with angels. He sent many strangers, that became like family, to love on him and care for him during every aspect of our journey. We became a blessing to them as well.

One of his CNA's had a son with the same name as his, but it was just spelled differently. Another used to attend our church when she was just a child, so she knew our Pastor and his family. She always made certain that Corion got enough to eat. She would fuss at me about coming in and cleaning him because it was their job, but I explained to her that I just needed to feel like I was doing something as his mother.

I would laugh when they would tell me stories about their experiences with him. The lady that cared for him in the mornings, Mrs. Sandra, said that he would yell out to her, *"Come here b****"* and she would say, "I'm coming Corion", as if that was her name. They would miss him so much when he would spend days or weeks in the hospital. They called after I took him home to check on him, during the pandemic because they missed him so much.

You have to be careful how you treat people because you never know how you, or your son, daughter or parents may end up needing that same level of care. The word says that we may be entertaining angels unaware. I honestly believe that was the case with Corion. He was God's angel in disguise. Really disguised. LOL

I would often joke with him that he was a great test for new CNAs to see if this were really the job for them. He surely put their patience, endurance, strength, and knowledge to the test. If you can pass his test, then surely you are ready for the job.

He definitely tested me when he got home. I wanted to give up so badly. But I knew I would worry even more about not being able to see him during the pandemic. I just cried out to the Lord to give me some relief. And He did. I especially remember one exhausting night when I sat out on my back porch to collect my thoughts and cry.

My sister sent me a text of some songs we listened to on our way to church when I was new in my faith journey. The songs took my mind back and I began to cry some more. I then heard the Lord tell me, "The devil is mad because you still have joy." He commended me for not losing my joy during this journey. I then began to praise God because truly I had joy. See joy is something the world can't give but will try to take it away. The joy is down on the inside. It's your strength in knowing that God has the last say about all situations.

Joy is different from happiness. Happiness is based on what happens, but joy can be defined as the opportunity between Jesus and you (J.O.Y.) I'd much rather have joy than happiness because I can still have my joy no matter the circumstances. To God be the Glory!

During our last stay in the hospital, he said to me, "*I am energy*." I wasn't sure what he meant by that, but I surely made a mental note of it. I did know that he could feel the energy of your spirit and countenance before you even entered the room.

Recently, I was listening to an old video interview of Dr. Sebi and he said, "You cannot kill energy; it's displaced from one state to another." That may be why it stings me when someone says that Corion died. I feel like his spirit still lives because I can feel his energy.

I have taught my grandchildren to say that he passed away, or that he went to heaven. I like to refer to it as his transition, or departure. I believe he is energy, as Dr. Sebi described, "displaced from one state of being to another."

He was keenly aware that he would one day leave this earth and he was good with it. He always told me that he knew more than I knew. I didn't really believe him nor understand him at the time, but now I am assured that he knew what he was saying in those moments. He knew that everything we had faced was necessary. It was all necessary.

So, when the doubt and questions of why wells up inside of me, I can still see him sitting in his chair in the driveway of our house on that nice spring Saturday afternoon. He was so peaceful and concise with his words. He knew his fate. He knew God's will for his life. He knew his purpose. He knew more than I knew.

Actually, that was another answer to my prayers for my son. I wanted him to know God and be assured of His love for him. I wanted him to know his purpose and God's plan for his life. I wanted him to live out God's will for his life. I honestly believe that in doing this we are assured of receiving the promise of everlasting life. This life is temporary and our bodies here on earth are temporary. Eternal life should be the goal.

Chapter 20

Who are you Mother?

"God is in the midst of her, she shall not be moved; God shall help her, just at the break of dawn." Psalms 46:5

During these six years, I believe the most significant thing for me is God teaching me who I am. Many times, Corion would ask me *"who are you mother?"* I would always laugh at that question, because I'm like, you know I'm your mother, cause you said "mother", so what are you asking me? Maybe he was asking, "who has God created you to be other than my mother?"

I especially remember the morning I was sitting on his bed, and he said to me, *"Ask Him to show you the mysteries about your life."* Wow, how specific is that! I had to get the bible to find scriptures that related to mystery (Ephesians 3:9; 1 Corinthians 15:51; Romans 16:25-26). The proper thing to do is to ask God what it means. God, who do you say I am?

Daniel 2:28 tells us that there is a God in heaven who reveals mysteries. Job 12:22 reads "He reveals mysteries from the darkness and brings the deep darkness into light." Also, Romans chapter 8 is vital to our understanding as children of God. I later listened to a sermon from, Stephanie Ike, called "Unusual Miracles". I was instantly drawn to her spirit and now consider her a friend in my head because I've never

115

actually met her. My sister in love Lisa shared this message with me after spending time with me and Corion over the summer.

Ike's message confirmed for me that there are mysteries God wants us to know about our life. Listening to several more of her messages opened my eyes to the fact that I had to face this spiritual battle alone. I had to be the one to fight the spirits within Corion. I had the authority, but I had to seek God for access. Once again, I had no idea what I was doing, but my faith was getting stronger as I got deeper into His word.

My Ancestor's Prayers

Bishop Jakes says, "Your destiny is always hidden in your history." In my study time, I noted we must learn to connect our history to our future to know who we are in Christ. I heard this saying during 2020 and I think it is a powerful statement. "I am the answer to my ancestor's prayers." Because someone else overcame, I am standing here today.

The book of Haggai chapter 1 gives a strong description of how life is for us today. It admonishes the audience to go into their house and "consider thy ways." While we are busy with our own house, His house lies in waste. His house is where His spirit dwells within me; my heart, mind, body and soul. This is confirmed in Acts 7:48 which states that the Most High does not dwell in houses made by human hands.

The passage describes how the people feared God enough to begin work on building a new house. Again, in Isaiah 26:20, we learn of the people instructed to go into their houses before impending judgement. Since the 2020 quarantine, through the leading of the Holy Spirit, I continue to work on my spiritual house in preparation for the coming of the Lord.

You Strong?

Corion asked me in the summer of 2014, *"You STRONG? You gone have to be strong."* I didn't know if he meant physically or mentally, but I felt like if I wasn't, I could be. In 2018, when he was ready to go, as he said, he told me to *"Be strong."* Then, in the hospital in 2020 he said, *"You STRONG. You strong as hell I swear to God you are."* He probably wasn't supposed to say that, but that's Corion. LOL! But he is a great reason for my strength because truly he is the strongest man I know. I also stand on the shoulders of many great strong women in my family, as well as those God has placed in my path.

Corion also said to me *"you are a beautiful mother."* He said, *"you are very incredible. I know you love me."* He didn't say all of these things at the same time, but God has put them together for me in my thoughts, in my heart, through my grief, and in my spirit, to strengthen me for my journey going forward without my soldier and the warrior, Corion.

In this journey, my focus was always on how I could "fix" or "repair" Corion's brokenness, but I eventually realized that it was my brokenness God was working to heal and repair so that I may complete the task he had set before me. That was another part of the plan, I just couldn't see it. I was told more than once; the trial was for me. The devil was after me, but I shunned that away because my love was focused on my child. It was easier to try to fix him, than to acknowledge my needs.

Restoreth My Soul

Self-care is vital for women. We often take on so many responsibilities and care for others, but we neglect caring for ourselves. I am thankful for those around me that know me well enough to remind me to take care of myself in times of stress. My husband shared with me very early in the journey, "You have to take care of yourself. You are the glue to this whole thing. If you break everything falls apart."

I was sure to take the time I needed to recharge and regroup as needed. As women, we must learn to save some of the love we pour into others, for ourselves. Many men have this figured out, while we've been labeled as selfish for doing so, but that's just a lie from the enemy. Save some of you for yourself, Sis. Trying to do it all is not realistic.

Corion even encouraged me to do so as well. He told me once when I came to visit him, "*You need to go outside.*" I laughed, but I was obedient to his request. We had our own language, and I knew exactly what he meant.

10/01/14 (social media post)
Corion: You alright? Me: Yea I'm OK. Corion: I want you to be alright. You need to go outside sometimes. Wow!! Still trying to take care of his momma. My boy! I love you Corion Dshawn Reed!

Mark 6:31
"Then, because so many people were coming and going that they did not even have a chance to eat, he said to them, "Come with me by yourselves to a quiet place and get some rest."

Listening to worship and gospel music, restores my strength. The word of God restores my strength. Listening to sermons restores my strength. During the pandemic, I needed my strength restored constantly. Some of my favorite speakers I enjoy listening to are Bishop T.D. Jakes, Pastors Sarah Jakes Roberts, Steven Furtick, Stephanie Ike, A.R. Williams, Priscilla Shirer and Kadesha Jenkins. They seem to speak to me directly. Their messages are always relatable to my circumstances and the way I connect to the word of God. He has blessed them that they may bless me. I feel connected to these people, and I've never even met them or spoken to them.

After Corion's departure, I felt strong spiritually, but I of course felt the loss. I needed to break down with someone who could help pour strength back into me. I needed a strong woman of God. My grandmother, mother and mother-in-law had already passed away. I needed strength and wisdom.

I called my First Lady, Missionary Ida Hamilton and asked if she was home. She said they were sitting outside and welcomed my presence. I quickly made it to her. I could already imagine myself falling into her lap. She was seated in a chair outside surrounded by family. I told her as I came up "Just let me do this." I fell to the ground on my knees with my upper body in her lap. I had finally learned how to be vulnerable in front of others. As I suspected, she cried with me and prayed for me as I let out all that I had been holding in as a mother that just lost her oldest child. God provided the person I needed to restore my strength in my time of sorrow. We should always honor and appreciate our elders.

My Mysteries

As I continuously write and share our journey, I find scriptures that strongly relate to our story. I was not completely clear about the "mystery" yet, but I knew that the Lord would tell me in due time. I now know, the mysteries of God can only be made known through spiritual revelation. His mysteries must be revealed through the Holy Spirit.

As I began to seek God for answers diligently, I was arrested in the spirit. I clearly heard, "You are God's daughter." Wow!! Knowing that I am a daughter of God has given me so much strength and a feeling of acceptance I've always longed for in this life. Sometimes you just need to be reminded and confirmed regarding who you are.

Galatians 3:26
"For you are all sons of God through faith in Christ Jesus."

Corion told me more than once, *"God loves you."* I'm not saying I'm special or different from anyone else. I surely have my own battles I'm still fighting. My life is nowhere near perfect, and I've made many mistakes. But I know that I am doing my best to maintain an open heart and mind to God's word, His leading and His will for my life.

In search of this mystery, I think back on my ancestry that I've been studying for many years. During the pandemic I learned a lot about my maternal great grandmothers. Many had the misfortune of losing a child. My great grandmother Mary actually lost a baby to whooping cough, and her adult son to a car accident. From my understanding, the family always felt the adult son's death wasn't an accident. But, to my understanding, they never pursued the issue. I grew up spending a lot of time with my great grandmother, and it helps me understand her more now. While many may have called her mean, I can now identify with her pain in some way. She was most likely masking her true feelings and it showed up as mean or onery. It was very likely that she wasn't mean, she was actually hurting.

My son said to me once, *"You are black and white. You are all white."* What in the world is he talking about, I thought? I soon learned that my paternal great grandmother, Martha's maiden name is White. She and my grandmother, Corrine, were actually good friends, which is how my mom and dad met. Now Corion's statement made sense that I am Black and White, but I am all White, because I married into the Black family.

It's also interesting that my lineage consists of colors. My father is a Green, and my mother is a Brown. Corion told me once, *"Come here with all those M&M's"*. The only thing I could find in scripture regarding colors was Joseph and his coat of many colors. Fast forward to when we were making burial arrangements. The representative was talking to us about the word of God because as I understood it, he is a minister. He started speaking about Joseph's coat of many colors. I was on the edge of my seat when he asked, "Do you know what the coat represented?" He was talking to my husband, but I was the one most interested in the answer. He said, "It represented God's glory." Wow. And as I often say, To God be the GLORY!

After listening to a Stephanie Ike sermon and thinking about Corion's words to me, I began to ask God to reveal the mysteries of my life. I began to declare and decree that I am who God says I am. I also began to understand that we must began to understand the authority God placed inside of us when He blew his breath into us before we entered our mother's womb. Stephanie instructed the listeners to write what God reveals to us, then declare it in our prayer time. She said, that if you tap into the knowledge of who you are, you will be the one in the position of power. I knew that I needed to be in that position to continue the spiritual battle that I saw before me at the time.

Then one day, God told me that my voice is to be used for God's glory. And that I am to become the words I speak before the Lord. When I was a child, I hated the sound of my voice. I can now recognize that it was the enemy that made me believe that I sounded like a man. That my voice was too deep. This was possibly why I would remain relatively quiet in school. Also, I didn't want to get in trouble because my mother did not play. LOL

Lastly, there must be something special about 12 years. Corion used to say *"Twelve years! Twelve looonggg years!"* I see the woman with the issue of blood had it twelve years, Jairus daughter was twelve, Jesus was twelve when he was found in the temple. There are 12 months in the year, Moses sent twelve to scout out the land in Canaan, and there were 12 disciples that walked with Jesus. Spiritually, the number 12 signifies perfection of government or rule.

God has a divine order, and the number twelve speaks to His divine order. He is placing all things in divine order in this season and maybe in a way we can now see. The enemy is normally hidden, but today many things are no longer hidden. The Lord is making full proof of His ministry in this season.

What I do know for sure is that we were all created to glorify God. God cannot be defined or restricted by our earthly understanding. He does things for His name's sake, for His glory. Whenever we are unsure with a decision, if we choose the thing that will bring glory to God's name, we are sure to make the best decision for ourselves and others.

Ephesians 2:10
"For we are God's handiwork, created in Christ Jesus to do good works, which God prepared in advance for us to do."

Chapter 21

Who you Blaming?

"Not rendering evil for evil or railing for railing: but contrariwise blessing; knowing that ye are thereunto called, that ye should inherit a blessing." 1 Peter 3:9

I can remember the night I went to see Corion, and he spoke to me in a vengeful way for the first time. I told him then, you are not my son because my son would never speak to me that way. I now believe this is the same spirit that caused him to bite Danielle on her face when she was pregnant with Jace. He was supposed to kiss her, but he clinched down on her cheek and would not let go. I was the one that encouraged her to allow him to kiss her when she was hesitant.

I really wanted to hurt him, but I had to look past what I thought he could understand and see his need just as God looks beyond our faults and sees our needs. Danielle was so calm and handled it with such dignity. She knows that it wasn't her brother's intention to hurt her. Isn't that beautiful! She is okay now and in time she healed, but the depth of love she showed in that moment will stay with me forever.

I can recall Corion asking me many times, *"Who you blaming?"* I would be puzzled because I didn't think I was "blaming" anyone for anything. But when he asked me, *"Who are you blaming now?"* I knew I had to search my heart for the answer. I was blaming him for not taking care of himself, I was blaming myself for not knowing what to do to keep this from happening (though there was nothing I could have done), and I was truly blaming others for not being there to support us.

But I soon realized that all those things were not meant to be. This journey and those that were there with us was in God's plan. Anything outside of that would have just been a hindrance or distraction. God had everything in His divine order.

It is often said that forgiveness is not for the other person but for you. It gives you relief as much as the other person. Love not only benefits others but it also helps to heal the broken places in your heart. Do unto others as you would have them do unto you. Treat others the way you want to be treated, because essentially it benefits you. And just as God always does, your story, as our story, will touch others and the love and benefit will be shared abroad.

I have forgiven those that I thought should have been there. I've even asked some to forgive me because I was truly angry with them in their absence. But I do realize that we must face the Father blameless. And I dare not go through all that I've experienced to have unforgiveness keep me out of the gates. Forgive whoever you must forgive so that we can make it into the kingdom together.

God will separate you and set you apart so that you may hear from Him. He requires your undivided attention. When He places me in these moments of separation and discipline, I've learned to say, "Lord I done got in your business again ain't' it? I'm so sorry." LOL

We often sit and dwell in regret for not doing a thing in hindsight, but if you could have understood things then the way you can see it now your response may have been different. But you must first have the experience, to do it different. Then consider some experiences you go through are more for others that come after you. They learn from our growth. That is how God works.

Accountability

Nevertheless, I finally learned in caring for Corion at home that I couldn't change him. He was who he was and how he was, so who am I to expect a person with an anoxic brain injury to respond to me in a manner that is not within his control? **Light bulb moment.** Can we truly expect people to respond to something they are not aware of?

So, I decided that maybe God is trying to show me something or teach me something. I began to seek God diligently. I went into my "upper room". The upper room represents a place of prayer; a secret quiet time and place where you prepare for the habitation of the Spirit of the Living God.

I asked, "Lord, what are you trying to show me?" The Holy Spirit let me know he was trying to show me MYSELF! I realize now that I raised my voice and punished my children far more than I should have. Looking back, I can see now how they operate in that spirit of anger and aggressive behavior. It's what I was taught and now I've passed it on to them to pass it on to their kids. I really didn't want it to continue. I began to repent, pray and seek God to break this generational curse before it goes any further down the line.

Corion told me himself once in a fit of rage. He said, *"I am like this because of you."* God told me that the anger was me; I gave him that spirit. That made me so ashamed. But I had to see myself before I could change. God revealed to me a curse of anger that I had passed on to my son. It took me a while to get it but confronting this generational curse and the spirit of fear, will allow our family to root it out and stop it from passing to future generations.

He couldn't change who he was, but I could certainly, take accountability for my behavior and modify my response to the situation. So, I went on a quest to be "nicer" to him and not give him the reactions he was seeking. This worked for about two seconds (LOL.... not literally). What I didn't realize at the time was that I was dealing with a demonic spirit, and he was smarter than me. I now understand why Corion would often say *"I know more than you."*

After lots of prayer and many YouTube videos of Bishop Jakes' and other sermons, I accepted that I was truly in spiritual warfare. You can't fight spiritual wars with carnal weapons. The enemy is an expert with carnal weapons. We must become proficient in spiritual things. I had to learn how to put on the whole armor of God. This was how David was able to defeat Goliath. It wasn't about the size of the enemy, but about the power in the weapon given by God.

James 5:16
"Confess your faults one to another, and pray one for another, that ye may be healed. The effectual fervent prayer of a righteous man availeth much."

Chapter 22
You want to Win?

"The Lord will protect him and keep him alive, And he shall be called blessed upon the earth; And do not give him over to the desire of his enemies." Psalm 41:3

One evening, I was in Corion's room preparing him for bed as I had done every night since he had come home. He gave me a stern look much like a coach preparing his players for a championship game. He asked me, "YOU WANT TO WIN?" I was startled, confused and a bit amused. I said "Huh!" He asked again just as stern, "YOU WANT TO WIN?" I tried not to laugh or show my confusion and answered, "Yes"', cause I'm always up for a challenge. He responded, "YOU SURE YOU WANT TO WIN? I quickly wondered what the cost would be as well cause that *"you sure"* gave me cause to pause. But I felt like I didn't have too much time before the coach would yell at me again, so I replied with a hesitant "Yes."

As I was writing this book, I came across a journal entry on June 26, 2020, he said to me, *"You have a lot of wins."* I also found a Facebook post where he told me, *"He know you a winner."* Then, the week of his transition he said to me in a whisper, ***"You won."*** **To God be the Glory!**

But ultimately, there was a sincere moment with my son while we were home together in 2020, that fueled a fire in my belly. I was preparing him for bed, and he gently grabbed hold of my arm to get my attention. He looked in my eyes and spoke these words to me, *"Every day you go to heaven, and every night I go to hell."* I was speechless.

What did this mean?! What is it that I am supposed to do because, surely, I am not going through all of this for my son to go to hell every night! After I left his room, I cried. I had to go back into my secret place, my closet where I meet with God and asked, "What is it that you want me to do? Whatever it is, I will do it because, this feels like torment." I had to dig deep and diligently began to seek God for purpose and an answer. If Corion and God could keep showing up, then so could I.

After his transition, God began to reveal His glory to me in many ways. Many would interpret the word for me as I shared our testimony about his transition. It was so surreal and not anything like I had dreaded. We truly felt God's will has been done just as we all had prayed.

12/19/2016 (social media post)
Him: It's good to be alive (listening to Boyz to Men CD)
Me: It's good to hear you say that
Him: He know you a winner
Me: Who???
Him: GOD....He know you a winner
Me: WE are winners.... it's taken you to strengthen me. (later)Well we are living for the weekend. You know what this weekend is?
Him: MY BIRTHDAY
Merry Christmas Fam! May your Christmas be merry and bright!
Mines already is!

When Corion returned to the dialysis center after his cardiac arrest, the nutritionist pulled me aside. She said, "They told me that Corion was dead, and I told them, no he isn't." She went on to say, "I had a dream. In the dream, he was in the casket, and they kept saying he is dead, and you were holding the paddles (defibrillator) against the casket saying, "No he ain't, no he ain't." Wow! I guess God showed her my fervent prayer.

Another time when we were in the hospital, I overheard the spirit inside of Corion saying, "She loves him too much!" They wanted to kill him, but his mom loved him too much. Love covers a multitude of sin. We can't go by what our eyes can see in life, or even what emotions we may feel. We must genuinely trust and believe God's word and walk blindly in agreement with His will for our lives.

2 Corinthians 5:7
"For we walk by faith, not by sight"

I had a dream also. I was sitting at a large brown table, and there was someone behind me holding a dirty blindfold over my eyes. Another was sliding a folded piece of paper in front of me as if I were to agree to this contract blindfolded. There were others in the room. In the dream it didn't feel like an agreement that I should have been agreeing to.

Many times, we walk blindly into agreement with the devil not knowing the consequences of our choices. We just go along until we get into a "situation". We then need the Lord to help us out of it and get angry at Him if he doesn't fix the mess we created. Why can't we choose to trust God in the same way? We must always pray God's will be done, concerning all matters.

There will be test and trials of life. Nothing worth having will come without pain. Jesus had to shed his blood and endure pain so that we might be free. Howbeit that we will be able to live this life without having to endure tribulation. We should take comfort in the fact that even in times of trouble, the Lord promises to be with us.

1 John 16:33 "I have told you these things, so that in me you may have peace. In this world you will have trouble. But take heart! I have overcome the world."

Knock at the Door

God gave me a dream of someone knocking at the door. In the dream, I could even hear Corion say, "front door open", like he does when our security system is triggered when the door opens. It seemed so real that I got up from the dream to check the door, but no one was there. I laid down and dreamed it again. In the dream there was a lot of tape covering the doorbell, both long and short tape strips. My reality was that I had repeatedly added tape strips to the catheter on Corion's thigh the night before.

This dream let me know that God was trying to do something, and I didn't want to answer the call. I was trying to muffle the sound of the "knock at the door" with the tape. It was time to let the catheter go. I knew if I let that go, as scary as it felt, He would move us into the next phase. And He would answer my prayers.

The answer wasn't what I was expecting but it was God's will. The doctors at the access center were able to replace the catheter once more, but not with much confidence that it would function properly. I knew it, and they knew, it was time to stop trying. I wasn't sure what was next, but I did know that I would have to trust that God had a plan. Corion had told me in June, *"God has a plan."* The following day, the Holy Spirit said to me, "The devil has schemes, but God has a plan."

I wasn't sure of the plan, but I was excited to see how He would get us out of this one. Whenever we faced a difficulty, I had gotten to a place where I would say, "Lord, I can't *wait* to see how you fix this." Many times, we stood at the brink of "there is nothing else we can do". But every time, God made a way out of no way.

As I understood it, most people that use a groin catheter don't make it long without getting infections and pass away shortly thereafter. Corion had his catheter almost 2 years, with no confirmed infections from the catheter. That was another miracle.

I felt some comfort with it when one of the nurses at the rehabilitation center said that her husband had a groin catheter and it had been over 1 year. That gave me so much relief, especially coming from the hospital with no knowledge of what to expect. God always had a ram in the bush to calm my nerves and fears. He is always so good to me! This was another reason my faith was constantly strengthened.

After having the dream, and having that last replacement catheter, I just had to wait for the next assignment. The doctors at the dialysis clinic suggested another procedure, but it would have been a daily regime and it would be as if we were both on dialysis, because I would be his sole caregiver. But if this is what God was leading me to do, I was willing to do it.

Revelation 3:20
"Behold, I stand at the door, and knock: if any man hear my voice, and open the door, I will come in to him, and will sup with him, and he with me."

Spiritual Weapons

God will always use something you already have within you. There are spiritual weapons within us we must learn to use for spiritual battles. I truly believe in this season He is teaching His people how to fight another way. I believe I had to first be in true relationship with the Father to hear his voice for instruction.

The first weapon God taught me to use was praise and worship by way of music. Music is a weapon used to attack the enemy to drive forces out and away. Music can affect what we cannot see or control. I often used it in the beginning as Corion's therapy and to bring joy, and that was good. But I later learned to use it as a weapon against the enemy's attack on me and him.

The music would help to arrest the spirit, but not until I understood it's power. I knew I could change the atmosphere through music. After he came home to stay, I had to learn how to usher in God's spirit to calm his mood and bind the unclean spirits. I would play music in the mornings before he went to dialysis. He enjoyed it so much. He would say loudly, "*Sang Ma!*" as if he really enjoyed it. But I also know God's presence was there as we worshipped.

The Holy Spirit, through God's word, said you must pronounce things before you go forward. We must be careful not to continue to repeat negative sayings and declarations. Instead, we can choose to respond with the opposite. We reject it and turn it back to those that sent it. Proclaim we are children of the living God with an invisible shield surrounding our home and our person put forth by the generals and watchers of God's army.

Wherever you are led by the Holy Spirit is where you have authority. We wrestle not against flesh and blood, but against principalities and darkness in high places. There are angels assigned to the churches and cities. To be effective, I had to determine the assignment of the principality in Corion. We are called to a territory and must go to the places where God sends us.

I've learned through my years of teaching from Pastor Hamilton about access to the ability to speak in tongues, or some may call praying in the spirit. When you pray in the spirit the bible calls it a perfect prayer. Allowing the Holy Spirit to speak for you allows you to reach God in a way that you can't in the natural. Where the anointing is the power of God shows up. You have access to dispel the lies about you and know who you truly are in God. The anointing is drawn to battles because it is the power of God.

The knowledge of God, the word and who you are builds courage. Courage is required when facing the spirit of fear. The truth of God's word, the truth of who God is, and who you are in Him gives courage to stand when you would otherwise retreat.

Ephesians 6:13-18
Wherefore take unto you the whole armor of God, that ye may be able to withstand in the evil day, and having done all, to stand.
Stand therefore, having your loins girt about with truth, and having on the breastplate of righteousness;
And your feet shod with the preparation of the gospel of peace;
Above all, taking the shield of faith, wherewith ye shall be able to quench all the fiery darts of the wicked.
And take the helmet of salvation, and the sword of the Spirit, which is the word of God:
Praying always with all prayer and supplication in the Spirit, and watching thereunto with all perseverance and supplication for all saints;

Chapter 23
His Purpose

"I cry out to God Most High, to God who will fulfill his purpose for me." Psalm 57:2

Corion had been having trouble with his dialysis catheter for the past several weeks. On Friday, August 28th, he was transported to the hospital because his leg was swollen, and he just wasn't himself. We were still in the pandemic, and I wasn't sure if they would allow me to stay with him at the hospital again, but my God is faithful. He had made the crooked places straight for me many times so I prayed that this time would be no different.

The plan was to put in a different access to do dialysis at home through his stomach. I wasn't looking forward to this at all, but if this was the next step, then I knew that the Lord would see us through it. I was hopeful that his surgeon who had been so good with him during past surgeries would be on call. I secretly made a pact with the Lord that if this particular doctor were doing the surgery, then that would be my sign that this was the right thing to do.

Prayers from all over the world

Corion was always curious, charismatic and wise beyond his years. Grown-ups would confide in him at a young age. As a teenager, he would advise his friends as if he was the adult in the group. They called him the young man with the old spirit in the barbershop because he would stay and talk to the old men after his haircut.

Just as we all do, he had his share of issues, especially anger, but he was also a gentle, caring and loving young man. He loved making friends and considered many to be like a brother. He was this way even as a child.

Corion had a way of bringing people together, and I always liked to refer to him as the life of the party. He was truly an unforgettable spirit with a big personality and a giving heart. I can still recall saying to him in 2014, while he was on the ventilator, "Boy you have people all over the world calling your name out to the Lord." Then I received a phone call or message from his friend that played basketball in Dubai. He wanted us to know that he was praying for him from there. Yep, just like I said, prayers from all over the world.

01/31/2014 (social media post)
Corion Reed has always had the spirit and charisma to bring a group
of ppl together. Oh how he has gone above and beyond this time. Your
prayers and your faith has strengthened and renewed mine. THIS IS
IN GOD'S HANDS AND NOT MAN'S which includes me. Today
my prayer and fast is for a sign. Lord give us a sign. We need a sign.
Please join me in this prayer and fast if you will.

Deuteronomy 3:22 (NIV)
"Do not be afraid of them; the LORD your God himself will fight for you."

I'm in Charge of the Circles

A circle is a sign of eternity; it has no beginning and no end. While we visited the hospital in August 2020, for the last time, Corion said in a proud childlike manner, *"I'm in charge of the circles. It's my purpose. It's been my purpose all my life."* I was just amazed that he could clearly articulate his purpose. I didn't know what it meant at the time, but I was surely proud.

Now this didn't make sense to me, but I've always been a writer. I got that from my mother. I created a photobook, *"My Kidney Story"*, for his birthday in 2011 after his transplant to remind him of what he had gone through. He was so proud of that book, he kept it in his car to show to others. I'm told it has been a blessing to many.

Similarly, I hope to write this memoir to remind our family and others of the love that grew from this dark time. But more so, to share the past six years of Corion's life, the many things he said and how this experience has strengthened our family.

When we are going through things in life, we can't understand the purpose nor the plan. But, as I write down the words and recount moments, I can clearly see how one thing had to happen for something else to happen. Everything has a purpose and is a part of a greater plan. Sure, there are consequences to our actions, but God can take ashes and make something of beauty out of it. God is strategic.

I now understand how my blessings and pain are connected to someone else's deliverance. Pain plays an important role in the manifestation of the blessing. It serves as the sign that you are carrying something inside that is bigger than you. We have the victory through promise, but not without a fight and pain.

The strength of our family through this journey has been simply amazing to me. We have had so many moments of darkness and despair, but they now pale in comparison to the good times, laughter and love we've shared with Corion at the helm of it all. We were surrounded by the love of individuals all in agreement and anticipation of God's promise. Corion was in charge of that circle of witnesses that believed as we believed and wished us well along the journey.

We are all Connected

During our last few weeks together, Corion shared so many things with me. I guess he was still making up for lost time. One clear memory is our last visit to the dialysis access center. As he gazed lovingly at the nurses' station he said, *"Everyone is connected. We are all connected."* He said it in a way that now feels to me like he had completed his mission; the circle was complete.

I agreed, in many ways we are all connected. But in hindsight I can now see this statement expressed in two ways. His expression could have meant that all of us are somehow intertwined; just as expressed earlier, my breakthrough depends on those that came before me, and someone else's depends on mine.

Actually, his miracle, his living so selflessly through this journey, has strengthened me to share his story and continues to build my faith, which I continue to share to help others, who in turn share and help yet more people. Remember when he said, it's not for us, it's for others. Yeaaaa that way!

The other way I took his "connected" statement is that his work was complete. He had made all the connections he was destined to make. On the anniversary of his rebirth in 2020 he said, *"I came back because I have something to do. I know what I have to do."*

All the people that we have encountered on this journey are now connected to his story. They have been charged to share their experiences in his presence and the joy he brought to their lives. Thru this exchange, I hope that God's love and His will can be spread as far as it can possibly extend.

The Hardest One

When I called to check in with Robert on Monday, I noticed that he wasn't at work. You must understand that my husband doesn't just take off work. I asked for how long he would be off, and he responded, "For an indefinite period of time." He didn't explain why he had taken off, but surely he felt that he needed to. We were a few days from the surgery so there wasn't a need to, but he must have felt something in his spirit.

After speaking with Robert that morning, I could recall Corion waking up much earlier, or even the night before, saying out loud, *"Pop! He was the hardest one."* God honors agreement within the earth when it aligns with His will. We had all come into agreement in the hospital, in 2014, to keep him on the ventilator, and not let anyone speak negative in the room where he lay unconscious.

Now we had all come into agreement, Robert, Cory, me, Danielle, Crystal and even Jacori, that we would allow God's will to be done, as Corion chose to not move forward with dialysis. Jacori had said to me earlier, "Gigi, don't drive yourself crazy trying to take care of my daddy."

The others each told me separately over the prior weeks, "Do whatever you think is best." Robert was still hoping for a solution from the doctors. He felt as if there was something more could be done. He later expressed that maybe the years we spent trying everything we could, had been in vain.

Corion had been having so much trouble with the catheter, that we knew a decision was imminent. But Corion made the decision once we all came into agreement. The surgery offered was just not what he wanted for himself, nor for me. He made his own decision. He told me, "*I am a grown man. I'm not a child anymore.*" That was to say, he knew what he was doing.

He kept pulling on the catheter. I asked, "You want that out?" He said, "*YES!*" I said, "You don't want to do this anymore?" He said "*NO!*" I replied, "Well if we don't do this you may die." He said, "*SO!*". I had no response. I had to respect his wishes.

Physician Confirmations

After that conversation, they tried to do dialysis once more, but he would not let anyone touch him. The catheter would not work, and he did not want to do another procedure. After he acted such a fool and embarrassed me beyond report, I finally gave in and said, "We are done, we are done, we are done! He doesn't want to do this anymore." They tried to convince me otherwise, but under the circumstances, the lateness of the hour and the lack of confidence I had in the staff performing the procedure that evening, it was a NO for me.

The doctor came in the next morning and ask, "What are we doing?" I replied, "We are going home to be at peace." He said, "I agree. You've done all you can do Mother. And I want to say, you've done the best you can do, and you've done well." The doctor even reached out to hug me and told me that I had been one of the best caregivers he has encountered. After he left the room, Corion said, *"I'm soooo happy!"* I asked, "Why?" He said, *"I just am"*.

I reached for my phone to text my family in the group chat, and he said, *"Who are you calling?"* I was surprised that he knew that I was contacting someone. As I searched for the words to explain what I was doing, I replied, "I am trying to call them to tell them you are happy, so that they, they know…" He completed my sentence and said, *"it's the right thing to do?"* Surprised at his response, I said, "Yes". He said to me *"It's the right thing to do."* Wow! To God be the Glory!!

He later asked me, *"Do you feel some pressure off?"* I said, "Yea, I guess I do." You see, the last thing I wanted to do is have to make another life-or-death decision. I had placed that decision in God's hands in 2014. I didn't want to take that back again. But this wasn't my decision this time. It was Corion's decision.

I had turned to the window while talking to my sister on the phone, but he could certainly hear the cracking in my voice from the crying. He yelled out, *"Don't make me feel bad!"* I apologized and explained, "I'm a girl. We use our tears and y'all save yours. I'm ok." The next time I felt

142

the urge to cry, I hid in the bathroom. But there was no fooling this guy. He said, *"Ma, bring me your face."* I obliged. He held my hand and said, *"You are a beautiful mother. Give me a kiss. I like to hear myself say it."* I did as he asked and settled my mind for the next phase.

Chapter 24
Facing Death

"For to me, to live is Christ, and to die is gain." Philippians 1:21

Corion had made all the connections he needed to make. I assume the circle he was in charge of was complete, and now he awaited his way of escape. On Monday, August 31, 2020, I made a note at 1:50pm of the vision he shared with me. He had been asleep, but he woke up super excited.

He said, *"Ma! I RANNN upstairs! It's beauuuutiful up there! I hear myself. I see momma! There she go right there!"* I was so excited for him because he was so elated. I said, "Corion, you ran! You ran upstairs! That means you were able to use your legs and your knees." He said, *"Yea, I did, didn't I."* But his excitement for my revelation surely paled in comparison to what he saw "upstairs."

He asked, *"Come here, momma. Give me a kiss. I like to hear myself say it."* Later that same day, he said in a sad voice, *"They say I'm gone die. That's what they saying."* Of course, being his mom, I comforted him and reassured him that we all have an appointed time to die, but no one knows when. So do not worry. But I knew deep in my heart of the real possibility.

You see, God had given me a premonition also. It was in the form of a dream about a month or so earlier. I woke up one morning in tears because I had seen my mother. She was very tall and wore a long flowing robe. I was excited to see her and asked why she was there, but she did not speak but gave me a loving smile.

In the dream, she was standing at what appeared to be a wooden baby crib. Even though I could not see him, I knew in my dream that Corion was in the crib, and he wasn't a baby but an adult. She was draping the covers around him as if to swaddle him like a baby. I knew she was about to take him with her, and I asked where they were going. But she didn't answer me. I woke up with tears in my eyes.

I began to describe this dream to my husband. With tears streaming down my face, I suddenly knew what this dream meant. I said to Robert, "My momma is coming to get my baby. My MOMMA is coming to get MY baby." In a strange way, it was sad but comforting. I could not imagine anyone else better for my son to be with but his loving grandmother. She always adored him, just as much as he adored her. A grandmother's love. To God be the Glory!

At Corion's funeral, as the directors prepared to close the casket, they folded the white cloth draping over the body. I whispered to Robert, "That's what my momma was doing in that dream." The same way the director was standing at the casket was how my mother stood at that crib in my dream.

I knew in death he would suffer no more pain, discomfort, sickness or disease. He would not be here with us, but he wasn't happy living in his body, unable to walk, hang out with his friends, and as he told me, more often than I wished to hear, he couldn't have sex. Lord, he was not happy about that AT ALL. Also, one of my greatest concerns was the possibility of me preceding him in death, not knowing if anyone would be able to care for him in the way I cared for him.

I remember when Corion was in the first rehab facility, he clearly told me, "*I didn't get to get married.*" Corion knew even then what his future held. I was hopeful, especially at that time, that it was just a moment of lamenting, but it was truer than I could even comprehend at that moment. He was speaking into the future even then, but I didn't recognize it until now.

"On Earth?!", Tuesday, September 1, 2020

After telling the doctor we were going home to be in peace, the surgeon who was to have performed the procedure came in to see us. Even though the procedure was scheduled for the next day, he took the time to come by to speak to us. He was accompanied by, I believe, two others on his staff. The care and concern for Corion, as his patient, was always impeccable.

He expressed to me that he considered me to be a very special person. He said that it had been his pleasure to serve us. I was so glad to see him because I also had something to share. He was such a special doctor and had one of the best bedside manners I'd experienced in this journey. I shared with him that I had made a pact with the Lord that I would only move forward with the procedure if he were the one doing the surgery. Even though we couldn't reach him before coming to the hospital, after Corion was admitted, I learned he had agreed to perform the surgery. I thanked him for the extra special care, patience and attention he had always shown towards us.

I know he was sent to us by God. He shared with me during an earlier visit about a personal connection to our case because of his experience with someone close to him. I'm assured that he understood the patience and tenacity it took on this journey. He told me that I had a special place in heaven on that day. Today I wanted to let him know that I believe he does too.

I had also learned that he was one of the best vascular surgeons in Memphis. God will bring everyone to the right place at the right time for his appointed purpose. Corion told me, *"He has everything laid out."* He was right again.

After we got home that evening, Corion slept most of the day. I went in to check on him while I was talking on the phone to my best friend, Timikka. I was telling her how happy he was. Robert also recalls how happy he was when he got home. He was truly in a state of expectancy.

When I went into his room, he awoke and asked, *"Where I'm at?"* with such wonder. I replied, "In your room, at home.". He was terribly disappointed and exclaimed, *"ON EARTH?."* Wow!! This again proves to me that he was truly aware of what he was facing and fully anticipating leaving this earthly realm.

I have a video from December 2019, where he told me in the hospital, he was ready to leave. I asked if he was ready to leave the hospital. He responded, *"I'm ready to leave earth."* As difficult as it was for me to accept the fact that he would pass away, I was overjoyed by his perspective and desire to make this decision for himself.

I had always hoped I didn't have to decide again whether to keep him on a ventilator or resuscitate. It's hard trying to make decisions for someone else's life, especially your child. God allowed him to make his own decision. That was amazing and a blessing. He also anticipated what was to come. That was Christ.

Hospice, Wednesday, 09/02/20, afternoon

Corion was having a good day. We got him up and dressed. The hospice nurse was arriving, so I thought it would be only right for him to participate in the conversation. He had a very happy and pleasant disposition that morning. He was trying to be a part of the conversation. The irony of it was us discussing hospice and end-of-life measures.

We had talked about hospice once before back in 2019, but it turned out it wasn't time. Back then, the coordinator agreed when she witnessed how he had come back much stronger than he appeared just a few days before.

Today, he was so excited and happy. Robert even reminisced afterward that he was the happiest he had seen him in a long time. I also recall Corion being excited and speaking as the nurse and I were speaking. But I caught him saying, *"I'm small. I'm nobody. But this is going to go all over the country, all over the nation!"* The nurse was also complimentary of his joyful spirit.

I so vividly recall how his eyes followed Pop as he walked past the living room and into the kitchen in the "busy" way he does when he is in a state of concern. Corion saw him and searched his brain, trying to make the connection between his sight and his heart to find words to identify this man. He said, *"He is my loved one, my family member."* Once Robert came into the room, he sat on the sofa facing Corion. Seated upright in his wheelchair, he studied him and then said firmly, *"Daddy, I love you!"*

Robert responded, "I love you too, man." This, for me, was the beginning of the end of a beautiful love story. This was the feeling I was enamored with in this moment. It was the best way for me to explain how I felt. It was bitter but sweet. I was overwhelmed with wonder and expectation. You see, I know that God can do exceedingly abundantly above all we can ask or think. I knew the possibility of death, but I still believed in God for miraculous healing. God had promised me something extraordinary, and I was expecting just that, without knowing exactly what it would look like.

At one point, the hospice nurse had to comfort me as we talked about the arrangements. But as usual, God's spirit took over, and I began to comfort her. She shared that she had recently lost her mother. There was so much death at that time. We were all grieving at some point during that year. After we were finished, we decided to investigate sending Corion to a hospice house when the time came near, as we weren't comfortable with him passing away at home.

"He Not Scared No Mo"

After we escorted the nurse to her car, we prepared for Danielle and the kids arrival. Just before the time, a sudden spirit of evil fell upon Corion, and he began cursing and acting out. He had been doing so well. Robert asked him if he wanted his hair cut and he responded with a strong, loud *"NO!"*.

Danielle and the kids arrived, and he began to act out even more. Once I got him calm enough, I moved him into his room and left him for a few moments to gather himself. When I returned, he said, *"He cool, he not scared no mo."* I immediately assumed that he was referring to the evil spirit I had become so familiar with.

This was when I realized when he acts out and tries to fight, I was really seeing the spirit of fear. He went on to say, *"I don't know if I'm going to heaven or hell. I can't act like that. It's got to be a difference when you are young and grown."* He felt as if he was not supposed to be scared because he was grown.

I recently listened to a message by Pastor Steven Furtick of Elevation Church titled "Too Grown to Give Up". It continues to amaze me how God leads me to sermons that speak to the things Corion has said to me. The message passage was from Hebrews 11:23-29.

In the passage, after he had grown up, Moses refused to be known as the son of Pharoah's daughter. Instead, he chose to be mistreated along with the people of God rather than enjoy the fleeting pleasures of sin. Further in the passage, it explains how Moses persevered because he saw him who is invisible. That, for me, is another incredible revelation.

Corion choosing not to continue with dialysis was him choosing to see He, who is invisible. He chose something invisible because he saw something that others didn't. He saw something he desired more, when he *"ran upstairs"* in his vision. This gave him a greater strength that could now be seen.

After hearing of his fear, I reassured him that he was going to heaven and that we all are afraid sometimes. I comforted him that, "The knowledge of God helps us with fear." He said in surprise, *"Oh, I didn't know that. When I start cussing and getting scared say, 'Corion, come here right now.'"*

Then he shared this, *"You came all the way to Mississippi by yourself to get me!! Do you know how far that is?"* Then he said, *"You came all the way from Africa by yourself to get me! Do you know how FAR that is?"* With a beautiful smile he said, *"I know you love me! You are very incredible."* I replied, "God is good." He said, *"He is AMAZING!"*

God has not given us the spirit of fear; but of power, love, and a sound mind. (2 Tim 1:7). After I put him to bed, he said, *"I need to do this, and I want to do this. The kids are not going to understand."* I told him that we would help the kids. He soon relaxed.

A few moments later, the kids came into the room. They began to dance to "Watch Me" by Silento, and he laughed and sang with them. That was their last moment together. I am happy it was a fun memory for him and them. They didn't stay long. He soon began to rest and remained in bed the remainder of the evening.

2 Peter 1:3
"His divine power has given us everything we need for a godly life through our knowledge of him who called us by his own glory and goodness."

Chapter 25

Spirit of Fear

"For God hath not given us the spirit of fear; but of power, and of love, and of a sound mind." 2 Timothy 1:7

A simple Google search will show that 'Fear not' shows up in the Bible 365 times. Where else do we find the number 365? Days in the year. So, I guess we can conclude, every day we should strive to fear not.

Journal Entry 06/26/20

Tonight, we watched "Keep it Moving" by TD Jakes and everything he said spoke to Corion's situation. We prayed and rebuked the enemy, especially of fear. Corion said he is scared. The message brought out how past trauma can bring out fear and doubt that will paralyze and affect parts of your body. Jakes specifically named things that my son was having trouble with. Corion said, "the cookies too heavy" and he "too tall". I'm not sure what this means. But I told him he already had the victory when God restored his life. He was even responding and agreed that the message was speaking to him. He understood the message. We prayed and praised God together (12:09 a.m.). Looking forward. We will keep it moving. He said I won't see the cussing anymore.

Me and Corion's time at home during quarantine forced me to seek God more. I was extremely challenged by his aggression and anger. I wanted to understand it better in hopes of helping him to gain better control over his emotions. But that was my plan; it wasn't God's plan.

As I sought God more, I could then feel His presence stronger. In hindsight, I could see that it was a spirit of fear at the root of the aggression, which affected Corion and me as well. Once I recognized the spirit of fear, I felt like I had moved to another level in this fight. As my knowledge of the word grew, I began to recognize how much my fear subsided. My focus began to shift.

I heard a minister say, "The real change occurs in your life when the thing that you are believing God for becomes bigger than that thing you are afraid of." (YouTube channel Official Derik Faison - "When God Hides You"). When Corion said to me, *"Every day you go to heaven and every night I go to hell"*, that thing on the inside of me became much bigger. My faith began to overcome my fear. I had to dig deep to find the weapons God's word says that He placed inside of me to fight. Scripture tells us Greater is He that is within me than he that is in the world.

My Fight with the Spirit of Fear, Thurs, 09/03/20

On Thursday morning at about 4am, Corion, and I had a different experience than we had in past mornings around this time. This spirit tried to tell me that I had my chance, and he was taking over. He said I left my son to die. All lies of the enemy. He said, *"your only child."* So, I definitely know that is a lie. I tried to stay back and not get too close, but he caught hold of my shirt. I was able to get loose by bending down lower than the bed, and his hand could not sustain the pressure of the railing.

When we talked earlier, Corion told me what to say when he acted this way. I tried saying it, but it only made the spirit angrier. But he was also consistently vomiting each time I said the phrase. He threw up on the wall and all over the bed. It was a deep red color and more liquid than solid. I later looked at the phrase I had written down from our earlier conversation. I didn't say the exact words he told me to say, but I did recognize that it was an evil spirit full of lies, and I no longer feared in the way it wanted me to.

But in the moment, since I wasn't quite sure what to say, I decided to find a video of TD Jakes talking about fear. The YouTube video I found was called "Fear No Evil." The spirit finally went away. I know it went away because Corion began repeating Psalm 23 with the Bishop as he recited his message.

The phrase Corion had given me to say was, *"Corion come here right now!"* I equate the vomiting to him purging the spirit of fear and the toxins within his earthly body.

Journal Entry 03/04/21

Everything regarding control and bad behavior is rooted in fear. What are you afraid of? Confront your fears. God has not given us a spirit of fear but of power, love, and a sound mind. How does God speak to you? I hear his voice in song, scripture, sermons, and even in conversations with others. He will keep you in perfect peace whose mind is stayed on him. Respect that everyone is not in the same place spiritually and mentally. Acknowledge that some are controlled by an indwelling spirit that is rooted in fear. Those spirits will attack anything that comes against it. They are vicious, mean, cunning and deceptive. They require spiritual weapons, as carnal weapons will not prevail against them. Jeremiah 1: 19, "and they fight against you; but they shall not prevail against you; for I am with you said the Lord, to deliver you, declares the Lord." If the Lord declares it, then you can believe it will be done!! Many times in scripture, God says do not be afraid. Jeremiah 20:11 says, "But the Lord is with me as a mighty terrible one: therefore my persecutors shall stumble, and they shall not prevail; they shall be greatly ashamed; for they shall not prosper; their everlasting confusion shall never be forgotten."

As I began to see the aggression of the spirit had subsided, I decided to clean off the wall. I got a towel, water and soap. I moved the bed from the wall, and with my back to him, I began to clean up the mess. Corion then spoke to me in his natural tone and said, *"God loves you."* I looked back at him and said with confidence, "I know."

Love leads us out of places of fear. I now realize that God was not only delivering him from fear, but He was also delivering me from a place of fear. My deliverance was my ability to turn my back on the enemy in faith. I know God to be my refuge and very present help in the time of trouble (Psalm 46:1).

Sarah Jakes Roberts says, "We must starve our fears and feed our hope." Whenever I feel afraid, I've learned to read Psalm 91, and every day I say Psalm 23. Early on, God encouraged me to learn Psalm 23 and the Lord's Prayer (Matthew 6:9-13). I had always believed it was my assignment to teach it to Corion after his brain injury. I wanted him to have a word of comfort when I wasn't available. But I had to learn it myself first. I now know it was really for my benefit more than his.

1 John 4:18
"There is no fear in love; but perfect love casteth out fear: because fear hath torment. He that feareth is not made perfect in love."

Chapter 26

Child of God

"And not for that nation only, but that also he should gather together in one the children of God that were scattered abroad." John 11:52

Initially, I delayed fully registering Corion for hospice because I was still undecided. We had the meeting and signed the paper, but I had to give them a call to make it official. I knew for certain this was what he wanted, so I had to respect his wishes despite my feelings. On that Wednesday evening, I noticed that his breathing began to appear labored. I called the hospice nurse to get him officially registered. They also sent over an oxygen machine late that evening.

He slept most of the day on Thursday. I waited all day for him to wake up so that we could go outside for some air. I thought that may help with his oxygen levels. He didn't eat much at all and just slept. He was having difficulty breathing, but he wouldn't keep the oxygen on for long.

Cornbread Friday, 09/04/20 4:18 a.m.

Early Friday morning, Robert and I were both awakened to Corion coughing. He had been throwing up all earlier and wasn't able to hold any food down. He was trying to tell us something as he coughed and gasped for air. He said, *"Cornbread!"* We both thought, "Cornbread??" We had a cornbread muffin in a brown paper bag next to the stove from lunch my sister-in-law brought use earlier that day. It was the only thing left. Robert asked, do you want me to heat it up and I agreed. Corion took a bite of the bread and said, *"I wanted it, and God provided. All you have to do is ask."* Then he looked to his Pop and said, *"Ask God for what you want."*

I knew that message was for Robert. I left them so that they could talk alone. I had prayed and asked God to give him a word of comfort as I knew he was struggling with all we've been through to come to this point. He expressed to me his feeling we didn't pray for God's well to be done. But I surely had prayed that prayer, even if others hadn't.

Matthew 7:7
"Ask, and it will be given to you; seek, and you will find; knock, and it will be opened to you."

Corion's breathing was much better now, and I had been waiting for him to wake up all day. So, we took him outside for some air. Robert said, "But it is 3 o'clock in the morning." I didn't' care. Every minute was precious at this point. So outside on our recently remodeled patio, me, him and Robert had a general conversation. But before we went inside, we prayed. Robert had expressed to me earlier his feeling that we hadn't prayed that God's will be done in 2014. I know I had, but I wanted us to do it again to be sure. We all prayed together that night and specifically asked that God's will be done. We came back inside.

After we got Corion settled back in bed, I asked him if he was okay. He said to me, *"I don't know. Let me think about it."* So, I sat in his room and waited. He closed his eyes as if he had fallen into a deep sleep. Then something woke him up. I had to get close to hear him, as he was now speaking in a whisper. He said, *"Man gone do it."* I had no idea what that meant, but I wrote it down, just as I had begun to do more consistently since he came home.

Robert had already fallen asleep, and now Corion was peacefully asleep too. During these last few days, he would say, *"God loves you. I love you. Y'all love me."* Maybe he was debating the choice he had made. He didn't want to leave us, but he knew a greater love and life awaited him.

He called me FINE

Before Corion passed, he woke up threw up again. He was talking at the same time saying, *"He called me fine. I'm fine. I ain't been called fine all my life since I was a child. He called me fine."* I asked, "Is that good?" He gleefully said, *"It's wonderful!"* Then he said, *"Please call me a child of God."*

So, for me that moment said, he could have chosen to live, continue on and be fine, but he wanted to be God's child. He was ready to see the kingdom of God and truly live in His presence. He made a choice and we as a family made the decision to respect his choice. He had given us so much joy and time despite his ailments. He was ready to go. It would not have been right for us to try and hold him here any longer. That is another reason I have so much peace.

My sister Ericka and Jacori got in Friday afternoon. We were all in Corion's room when he forcefully asked, "She told him yet?" We all looked a bit confused. Surely, he wasn't saying what we think he was saying. I said, "Told him what?" He aggressively said, "BYE! Tell him!".

I was so annoyed. This definitely wasn't the way we wanted to break the news to his son. But I gently explained the situation, and Jacori seemed to be as understanding as he could.

We had a beautiful day on Friday. We had some visitors. His sitter Ms. Pat came to see him that afternoon for the last time. She did all she could not to cry, just as I had requested. He gave her the biggest smile when she came into the room.

He even allowed Robert to cut his hair. He gave a gentle response versus the strong "*No*" he had given on Wednesday. My very good friend Nancy and my husband's sister Laura came by to spend some time with us. Once again, he knew more than we knew that evening. He was quiet and observant.

Danielle came directly after work, but without the kids as requested. I could tell from the last visit that he did not want to see them again. He also allowed her to love on him way more than he normally would. He looked so handsome, as she gently rubbed his bald head. Surely, he was fully aware this would be the last time, as he ordinarily would not have allowed this amount of affection from his little sister.

Can't Cry

Corion woke up one night during the week of his transition and told Robert and I, "*I can't cry. I want to cry. I try to cry. But I can't cry.*" I didn't write it down, but I remembered it immediately when my grandson told me he couldn't cry. It was almost a week after his father's death, and I asked if he was ok, and assured him that it was ok to cry. That's when he said, "I haven't been able to cry."

I had become friends a month or more earlier, with one of Corion's social workers. We'd never met in person, due to COVID. She was a Godsend via phone one morning I was having a complete meltdown. It was one of those awful mornings trying to get Corion dressed, and he was being a clown, but more so than normal. I asked God, through my heaving tearful cry, to please help me. Then, the phone rang. It was her sweet voice on the other end that calmed me down. We became instant friends.

While I was sharing the news of Corion's passing with her, I told her how both Corion and Jacori had told me that they couldn't cry. She replied in such amazement, "I ain't no prophet, but we just had a bible study lesson this week and it must have been for you." She said, she didn't know about why my grandson couldn't cry, but Corion couldn't cry because God had already wiped away his tears.

Revelation 21:4
"He will wipe every tear from their eyes. There will be no more death or mourning or crying or pain, for the old order of things has passed away.'"

After studying the commentary on this verse, the wiping away of the tears is symbolic of God preparing Corion for a place where there would be no more sorrow or pain. It was assurance for me that God was preparing him for that beautiful place upstairs where tears were no longer necessary. Jacori's mom, Jasmine said, "It was confirmation that he is at peace." I love that!

Nothing Nothing Nothing!

During the last days of life, Corion woke up out of his sleep and so joyfully said, "Nothing Nothing Nothing"! I was reminded of this in my time with God one morning recently. The Holy Spirit said to me, "Nothing can separate you from my love." I am assured that this is what God was saying to him. I also can recall that he had expressed his concern as to where he would spend eternity, however, he also confidently told me often, *"God loves me."*

Romans 8:31-39 (NIV)
Nothing Can Separate Us from God's Love

What shall we say about such wonderful things as these? If God is for us, who can ever be against us? Since he did not spare even his own Son but gave him up for us all, won't he also give us everything else? Who dares accuse us whom God has chosen for his own? No one—for God himself has given us right standing with himself. Who then will condemn us? No one— for Christ Jesus died for us and was raised to life for us, and he is sitting in the place of honor at God's right hand, pleading for us.

Can anything ever separate us from Christ's love? Does it mean he no longer loves us if we have trouble or calamity, or are persecuted, or hungry, or destitute, or in danger, or threatened with death? (As the Scriptures say, "For your sake we are killed every day; we are being slaughtered like sheep." No, despite all these things, overwhelming victory is ours through Christ, who loved us. And I am convinced that nothing can ever separate us from God's love.

Neither death nor life, neither angels nor demons, neither our fears for today nor our worries about tomorrow—not even the powers of hell can separate us from God's love. No power in the sky above or in the earth below—indeed, nothing in all creation will ever be able to separate us from the love of God that is revealed in Christ Jesus our Lord.

Chapter 27
God's Will be Done

"Be strong, and let us show ourselves courageous for the sake of our people and for the cities of our God; and may the Lord do what is good in His sight." 2 Samuel 10:12

People could not understand my peace and overwhelming sense of joy in days following his transition, but it was because God allowed me to know His truth on a different level. He has given me an anointing that surpasses all understanding, even my own.

There are moments when I've grieved the passing of my baby, my son, my first-born child. But it doesn't last long, because of God's peace and the many memories Corion and I made together. I can still hear his voice and words of comfort. He assured me during his last days, *"I need to do this, and I want to do this."* He said, *"The kids are not going to understand"*, and that has been so very true.

I remember when he first began to speak again, he told me, *"I never got to get married."* That now tells me that he already knew then what the future would be for him. So, in knowing that now, it makes sense that he would say *"I know more than you think I know. I know more than you."*

I made a Facebook post on January 23, 2020, of him sharing with me that he came back for a reason. *"I know why I came back. I know what I have to do."* I asked, "What do I need to do?" He said, *"You did everything you needed to do, and it was good."* In God's word, He tells us to be good, not excellent. The world has put that strain on us, not God. I believe we stretch ourselves too thin trying to be something extra, thus cutting out the time and energy we should be spending doing God's will. He is looking for a good and faithful servant. I've learned to be okay with good because that is what pleases the Father.

Lost all my Clout, Saturday, 09/05/20 5:51a.m.

I went in to give Corion fish oil this morning so that he can have a bile movement, but the spirit was upset with me and said, *"I knew you was going to do that b******t! You want me to leave."* I'm confused, like what are you talking about. He said, *"That's what you are doing."* I said boy take this stuff. Then the spirit told me, *"I lost all my clout. I'm leaving."*

I sat back into Corion's wheelchair and said **"Corion, run for your life! He doesn't have any power over you! Run for your life Corion"**! I began to praise God and the spirit became angry and said *"I ain't going nowhere, I ain't going nowhere, bye, bye, bye, bye"*, but I praised God in the spirit and began to lift my hands to the Father. I opened my eyes to see Corion raising his hands and it was shaking with the touch of the Holy Spirit. He began saying *"Hallelujah"* along with me. He looked really good not to have had dialysis for one week.

His Preparation

Saturday morning, two CNAs from hospice came to bath him. I had cleaned him up earlier but when they asked if I wanted them to bathe him again, I looked at him and he nodded his head *"Yes"*. As I think back, he had his bath and a nice haircut. He was fully prepared to exchange his old house for his new garments. I later reflected on this moment as his preparation for the trip. The Holy Spirit led me to this scripture.

Zechariah 3:1-5
"Then he showed me Joshua the high priest standing before the angel of the Lord, and Satan standing at his right side to accuse him. The Lord said to Satan, "The Lord rebuke you, Satan! The Lord, who has chosen Jerusalem, rebuke you! Is not this man a burning stick snatched from the fire?" Now Joshua was dressed in filthy clothes as he stood before the angel. The angel said to those who were standing before him, "Take off his filthy clothes." Then he said to Joshua, "See, I have taken away your sin, and I will put fine garments on you." Then I said, "Put a clean turban on his head." So they put a clean turban on his head and clothed him, while the angel of the Lord stood by."

After the CNAs left, I had to make a quick trip to the grocery store. While sitting in the store's parking lot, I took the time to return a phone call to Jace's grandmother, Shelly. I was sharing with her all that we were experiencing and all its amazement and wonder. As we spoke, I could feel the Holy Spirit take over us both. She said to me, "Corion has been having conversations with God and trying to translate it to you the best way he can." She went on to say, "God doesn't speak our English language, but a heavenly language. He was doing his best, but it didn't all make sense to us."

I totally agreed with her statement. Before we hung up, she said, "Go home and tell Corion you understand what he has been trying to tell you. Tell him you get it." I was so excited by that conversation. But as soon as I walked in, Jacori was excited as well. He said, "My daddy called me. He said '*Come here. Come here*'. I went in and he opened his arms and wanted to hug me." I asked Jacori, where was he when his daddy called, because you must understand at this point Corion's voice was not much above a whisper. He said he was in the office several feet away from the room where Corion laid in bed on an oxygen machine.

That was an answer to my prayer. I had asked God to allow him to have a genuine moment with his son before he passed away. At the time, I could not understand Corion's toughness with Jacori being there. He had specifically asked for him before we came home from the hospital. As a matter of fact, we spoke to Jacori by phone one day we were there.

Jacori shared with us that he had been to Memphis, but he didn't stop by to see us. Corion responded without any prompting, *"I must not be a good daddy. You didn't come see me."* Jacori was just as shocked, as I was by this. He apologized and promised to come see him soon. So, when we were preparing to go home from the hospital for hospice, I asked if he wanted to see Jacori and he said, *"Yes"*.

After Corion's departure, the Lord revealed to me that Corion was putting on a tough exterior with Jacori. The Holy Spirit said, "It hurt him too bad baby." It was difficult enough to leave us, his sister, nephew and niece. But it was gut wrenching for him to know he was leaving his son. It was the primary reason he did not wait for Crystal as she had asked when he spoke to her by phone. He could hear her, he nodded his head, but his heart could not take the pain of her tears.

His Transition

After listening to the great news from Jacori, I went into Corion's room. His eyes were closed, but I knew that he could hear me. Just as Shelly had prompted me to, I said, "Corion, I know what you have been trying to do. I understand." Within minutes of that moment, Corion began to transition. He had several seizures. In between episodes, he spoke to his father, Cory, and the phone call with Crystal.

We were able to contact the hospice nurse who made it there quickly. We were frantically on the phone trying to arrange for the hospice house, but we soon found that there was no time for that. Between seizures he would be alert. There was one very hard seizure as, Robert had his hand on his head praying for him. Suddenly, his speech went from a whisper to normal and he said, *"That was a hard one. I ain't never felt that before."* It was as if he was released from something. It is my belief that it was his release from the stronghold. I remember when he told me earlier, *"Man gone do it."*

Robert left the room. I was sitting with Corion, and he said to me, *"He gone. I'on know what to do."* I said, "Let's pray the prayer of repentance." I had taped it to the wall, along with many other scriptures. I wanted to be prepared to say the right words whenever we prayed. We asked God to forgive his sin, come into his heart, and save him.

Within a few moments, he began to have a seizure again and I started calling him in the manner he had told me to do when he acted out. Corion said to me clearly, *"I ain't gone yet."* I could tell by his tone, that I was getting on his nerves, this wasn't the time to be calling him back, and he was ready to go. It was as if to say, "Momma don't call me back to this earth again." I said, "I'm sorry. I'm going to let you go." Only the two of us can possibly understand the strange humor of this moment. He soon departed this life in peace.

09/06/20 (social media post)

My baby got his wings yesterday He "ran upstairs to that Beautiful place" he told me about in the hospital last week and into the loving arms of his grandmother that he saw already there I'm soooo blessed to have been his mom because he was soooo AWESOME and loving and sweet....most of the time I am going to miss him so much, but he got to make his own choice and was so clear that I dare not deny God's will for him of everlasting life. He gave me confirmation at least 7 times. He was peaceful and so very handsome and oh so the strongest man I know I love him so much and I am so thankful to my village for allowing me to share our journey through this screen. I love you and I will always think of you and pray for you because you are now part of me. We are family. Corion taught me that To God be the GLORY! His praise will continue to be in my mouth for all He has done

My mom and my son were buried side by side 6 years apart. It wasn't planned but it was another sign from God that He had everything laid out like Corion said. God blessed me with His greatest gift......TIME!

Chapter 28

An Expected End

"For I know the thoughts that I think toward you, saith the LORD, thoughts of peace, and not of evil, to give you an expected end." Jeremiah 29:11(KJV)

I believe that God is doing a new thing. The world in 2020 is looking for the "new normal" because things have changed so much. Many are no longer able to do the things they've been accustomed to doing without having to be aware of the "consequences" of this virus. They are told that they are to blame if they go out without a mask. They are cautioned about their visits with their grandparents or vulnerable loved ones because they may not be able to live through the virus if they catch it.

For many years, many of the younger generation have watched while their loved ones "followed the rules" of the word. The results of the change is beautiful in many ways, but it does not yield the trouble-free life many anticipate. John 16:33, let us know, in the world we will have trouble. Yet we still expect to be trouble-free.

In 2014, I prayed for God to let my son live and be a testimony to His kingdom. God did just that! I asked and received; however, God did not choose to restore him completely to his previous state of mind, give him full activity of his limbs, nor the ability to live the life he had once lived. I even asked God, "Why did you have to take my son?" He said to me, "Because he wasn't yours, he was mine. And when the time comes I will take you home also."

From an on-lookers' perspective, it may seem that God did not answer our prayer. But I've come to know that God's ways are not our ways, and His thoughts are not our thoughts. The miracle that He showed us was so much greater than what our eyes could see.

When I go back through the videos, photos, and Facebook posts in 2014, I can clearly see what God was doing. I see the miracle and it is amazing. God healed Corion in 2014. His body may not have responded to the healing, but his soul did.

Corion knew who we were, he started feeding himself, and he responded appropriately in many ways. But it was the fighting spirit, fear of the unknown, inconvenience, and carnal expectations that kept me from seeing him the way God saw him.

God has taught me through this journey, not only did he restore Corion's soul, but He also restored mine. I pray that this will extend to many others. He used this young man lying in a bed, cursing, and fighting at times, to show many people how to give and receive unconditional love.

That is the character of God. We've learned the "rules" of the word, how to act, how to dress, how to tithe, how to speak, how to forsake. But have we learned how to get in God's presence? Have we learned how to seek Him diligently daily? Have we learned how to truly give to others when they don't seem worthy of what you give? Have we learned how to laugh together and cry together?

I wasn't ready for Corion to leave in 2014 and neither was he. But in 2020, he was ready, and I had the confidence that God was ready for him. He fought the good fight, finished the race, and kept the faith (2 Timothy 4:7).

Distractions

The word of God is very important. Every word is strategic and important because they give context. I've always quoted Jeremiah 29:11 as it relates to Corion. The last words of this passage in the King James Version reads "an expected end". As I go back through the things that I have written over the years, I can truly acknowledge that there was an expected end. It wasn't my expectation, but it was God's.

As I journaled June 20, 2020, the words, "unexpected end", came into my mind in the middle of my conversation with God. I didn't understand why, however I am so happy the Holy Spirit lead me to write it down as I completed the thoughts that poured into me. With a new understanding I can now identify this as, a distraction. These words contradict God's word. God's word promised an expected end, however the enemy tried to have me believe something different.

Words are important. They are what separate us from other living things on earth. The location of words, the tense, the tone, and sentence structure can alter your entire view of a situation and circumstances. When you change your words, you change your thinking, which will also change your life.

Words can be used to destroy an entire generation and/or nation. Words can insight fear or bring comfort. Words can build up or tear down. Words can discourage or encourage. Words give life and words can kill. Words are a powerful weapon. The Word of God is the most powerful.

God has a plan for our lives. He has a purpose for us all. Nothing is wasted. Everything you've gone through in your life is a part of His purpose and His plan. My sister told me today about friends she has been able to encourage that have lost their mother that they have cared for in their fight with breast cancer. Had she not experienced firsthand caring for mom after surgery with changing the dressing on her wounds, cooking her meals, and witnessing her sudden death, she would not be able to help others that now need her knowledge and compassion with that experience.

Chosen

I remember stopping for lunch with Corion in 2009 after a doctor's appointment with the nephrologist. He was ordering a sandwich and being very selective about what he could not have on the sandwich. He was trying to stick to the renal diet recommended by the doctor. The lady in line behind him must have wondered why this young, strong and healthy-looking man was so particular about his sandwich. She dared to ask, and he so kindly told her about his recent diagnosis. She then confidently told him, "You are chosen. God has trusted you with this." He replied, *"I never thought about it that way. Thanks."*

During the year 2014, I was really wanting to give up, and my husband gently said to me, "We don't' have a choice. We have to keep going." Then just the other day, Nancy, and I were talking. She said, "I didn't choose my gift." I responded, "Then it was chosen for you." It's my belief, circumstances we don't choose for ourselves, can be the thing that God has called us to, so that our lives may reveal Him to someone else. Consider this. When God doesn't change your circumstance, He will change *you* for the circumstance. But it's up to us to acknowledge Him and choose to be obedient to the call.

Matthew 22:14
"For many are invited, but few are chosen."

To be chosen is to be trusted with a choice. Being chosen by God is to be trusted with a responsibility to choose the things of God to fulfil the purpose He has laid before you. He knows what he has placed inside of you. He knows the incredible things you are capable of through His guidance and permissive will.

In the earthly realm, most people consider being chosen as receiving more privileges. However, in the spiritual realm, it is quite the contrary. It is a responsibility that requires standards to do God's will and make the daily choice to honor a covenant. Most times things are subtracted when you are chosen, so that God's glory may be revealed.

Being chosen by God for a task is truly an honor, however, we must also remember that it is not without sacrifice. It is a privilege to be trusted to complete a mission much greater than yourself. Yet, it is still a choice. You must choose to honor the mission. You must choose to move forward in obedience to His word and instruction, even when it is difficult. You must choose to accept the difficulties that come with the obligation, trusting that it is for a greater good that you may not see in your time.

I've always felt honored that our family was chosen for this journey. Despite the challenges we've faced, I've seen perseverance with a growing sense of love and purpose. I've witnessed not just myself, but also others in our family continue to encourage, support, and minister about God's love to many. The encouraging words from others has also helped to fuel us through this mission.

04/03/2017 (social media post)
Yesterday, like many days before it, was a mental struggle for me. I don't have the words to explain it to others, so as best, I talk to God about it. As I pressed to do what was desired, I was comforted by God's confirmation to our conversation; Corion sleeping peacefully when I left him. He understands my struggle and continues to supply my need. God sees, He knows, He understands, He cares, He answers. Thank you Lord for being ever present in our lives.

Michele Lynnette (post comment)
See I could actually feel you while reading this...... Many of us can only sympathize with you because we have not walked in your shoes...But having to be there for Corion, oversee his living conditions, making decisions and handling things with his health, be a VP and high decision maker on the job, be a wife, mother and GiGi at home while you think about your other child on the other side of town, attend community events for both personal and business and then still try to LIVE LIFE!!!! WHEW!! I can only imagine how heavy your load gets BUT God knew you were the "Job" for the task........Whether it feels like it or not, you are headed for the other side of THROUGH!! It may feel like you're just treading water at times but you're moving!!!! It's a great reward and blessing on THIS SIDE OF THIS TEST!!! LORD I FEEL MY HELP!!!!!! If some days you don't feel like running, walk. If other days you don't

feel like walking, crawl!! But just keep moving cuz you're on your way!!!!!

John 15:16

"You did not choose Me, but I chose you and appointed you that you should go and bear fruit, and that your fruit should remain, that whatever you ask the Father in My name He may give you."

Not by Design but Usable

On 07/21/20, I made my last journal entry before his passing.

I've not been writing but God has still been pouring into me. I had a moment yesterday that was like a title "Not by Design but Usable", or something like that. I purchased my favorite Lysol toilet cleaner from Dollar Tree. I was excited to see them because they are usually pretty expensive in the grocery store, and I can get them for $1 each. I was introduced to them by my brother-in-law when he lived with us for a brief moment. Love him because he cooked and cleaned. He was a great house guest.

Anyway, I went to add it to my freshly cleaned toilet and the plastic that holds it to the toilet broke. Just snapped. So of course I assumed this is why it was $1. Also for a brief moment thought just to throw it away because it wasn't going to work as designed. But then I thought to open the top to the toilet tank and drop it down into the tank. Same result if not better. Now the water has the cleaner already marinated in it before it goes into the toilet bowl.

Not by design but still usable. God makes us that way. We may not be what others expect, but we can be used by God and be as effective, if not more effective. I may not have gone to seminary, but I do hear from God and can share

His word with others. Corion may not be able to stand before people and preach a sermon, or even tell his testimony, but God has truly blessed his life through this journey to help others.

1 Samuel 16:7 (NIV)
But the LORD said to Samuel, "Do not consider his appearance or his height, for I have rejected him. The LORD does not look at the things people look at. People look at the outward appearance, but the LORD looks at the heart."

Chapter 29

God's Timing

"Come now, you who say, "Today or tomorrow we will go to such and such a city, spend a year there, buy and sell, and make a profit", whereas you do not know what will happen tomorrow....Instead you ought to say, "If the Lord wills, we shall live and do this or that." James 4:14-15

Thinking back on the beginning of our journey, we sat in the hospital with Corion more than a month. Nothing else mattered. Our jobs, our house, the bills, the cars, nothing. We only focused on him and helping one another cope with the current situation at hand. This is where the change in our relationships began. This is where I began to learn patience. This is where we learned to focus on the things in life that truly matter. This is where we began to learn how to truly trust God for all our needs. This is how we have chosen to live; in a posture of faith, prayer, gratitude, expectancy, and love. To God be the GLORY!

Impatiently Waiting

God will put us in places where we can clearly see what really matters in this life. All the distractions are halted, as we must gain focus and look to Him for relief. Patience has always been a challenge for me. However when I consider that many in my generation were groomed by 30-minute sitcoms to think we can resolve problems quickly, it makes sense. The next generation grew up with a microwave, believing food can be cooked quickly with a very short wait time, as well as 24-hour television programming. The newest generation's attention can only be held at the rate of 30-45 second sound bites and TikTok videos. There is no time attached to solutions and understanding, and therefore we perish for a lack knowledge. With the shutdown of the world in 2020, we were blessed with time with our families, but for many it felt like a curse.

11/19/2015 (social media post)
"PATIENT PATIENT PATIENT, I'm so sick of that word!" I know
how you feel Corion Dshawn Reed! Me too!!!

My experiences with Corion at home in 2020, felt as though it moved at turbo speed; like it was on steroids. But Corion said to me one day when I was getting him dressed, *"You on time now."* I guess I had to play catch-up from when I was pouting a few years back and refusing to go forward because things were not working out in the way I thought they should go. I was wasting time. And he knew it.

But now, this time at home, gave me time to truly focus on the things God was doing in our life. 2020 was a year of great trials and tribulations for the masses, but God also blessed many to grow from this time and flourish. I began to seek Him earnestly concerning the current circumstances we were all faced with. I had more time than I'd had before and wanted to use it properly.

I knew there was something special about the year because Corion had told me at the beginning of the year in January that he knew what he had to do. I also know in April, God told me it was time for me to bring him home and that he needed me now. I often tell people that in 2020, God shut down the world for me!! It gave me the opportunity to care for my son and work from home. Two things I've longed for many years. He allowed me to spend precious time with him, so that I could hear what he was trying to share with me. These were our last moments together. I didn't know it, but God certainly did.

Since we began this journey, we acknowledged the value of time as we had a consistent reminder. We quickly learned that time is fleeting, and we must make haste to move when the spirit says move. God doesn't give suggestions; He gives commands; therefore, we must obey immediately because the window may be closing.

I later learned that our obedience is not only for our benefit but also for the benefit of others. Your blessings are tied to your obedience and those blessings are also for the benefit of others. We must move before the door closes, and to avoid, not only delaying our blessing, but the blessings of others. Consider also that our disobedience may be holding up someone else's breakthrough or healing.

2 Corinthians 10:3-6
"For though we live in the world, we do not wage war as the world does. The weapons we fight with are not the weapons of the world. On the contrary, they have divine power to demolish strongholds. We demolish arguments and every pretension that sets itself up against the knowledge of God, and we take captive every thought to make it obedient to Christ. And we will be ready to punish every act of disobedience, once your obedience is complete"

There will be Trouble

We are mistaken in thinking that a life in God will be perfect and without trouble. We are unable to earn His love, nor live up to deserving a life in heaven. We are flawed and imperfect. We are human. We make mistakes, we express and act out of emotions, we get confused, we don't understand, we make bad decisions. We become impatient in waiting and have a strong desire to give up along the way. But what I have learned is that if we develop a genuine relationship with God, through acceptance of Jesus and the Holy Spirit, we will be changed from the inside out to become more of who God designed us to be.

Our lives are not just about us. The timing of our breakthrough, or miracle is connected to someone else's. Someone, somewhere unknown to you, is waiting on you to overcome what you are dealing with for them to live. This should show us how much we need one another. This is where true love for your fellow man may well begin.

Time is a Gift

We live in time, while God exists in eternity. He created time so that we could learn to appreciate life. Our answers to life's mysteries are in eternity. Psalm 90:12 states, "Teach us to number our days, that we may gain a heart of wisdom."

I've learned not to be so distracted by the things I don't have, as it will very well make me miss the things I do have. What we have now is time and time is a gift. We often try to catch up on sleep or make up time lost with children when they were young. But once time is gone, it is gone. It must not be wasted because we cannot get it back. We must appreciate time and use it wisely.

The Lord holds time in His hands, and it is a gift to us. God is not controlled by time, yet He controls time. Times and seasons belong to the Lord. It is a gift to us that we must work harder to appreciate and treasure. That's why time is called the present. I am ever so thankful for the additional time I was blessed to have with Corion.

Time is precious, but we often don't know how precious it is until it comes to an end. Time is what God gives us, in exchange for our faith in Him. He controls the time while we must continue to act in faith. The promises of God are not based on our timing.

We try to add to ourselves through external means, when honestly all of what we need for this life is already inside us. We must learn to access it through the Holy Spirit and be patient. One of the hardest lessons is patience. But patience is a virtue. What is a virtue? It is a gift from God. And once you've waited for the thing you wanted most, you'll realize sometimes that the wait wasn't long enough because we are still not ready when the time comes. Even after 6 years of many challenges with Corion and wanting the struggle to end, the timing of his passing now seems way too soon.

James 1:4
But let patience have her perfect work, that ye may be perfect and entire,
wanting nothing.

Journal Entry 02/9/21

You'll have moments that you remember but think are unimportant but later find He was building you. He was answering you; He was giving you results without you even knowing it. Because if He does it all at one time, you'll soon forget. After mother's give birth, in time that, labor pain is long forgotten, and later becomes an unruly teenager. Those sacrifices of losing weight down the line turn into stress eating.

He knows the cares of this world will cause us to lose focus and get off track, but He has taken you thru the small victories because they will later become the weapons you need to fight the real battles. We are in a spiritual war. He has taught you how to fight by taking you thru many small victories. Recall them and how you came thru victorious. What did it take? Determination, prayer, sacrifice, courage, pushing thru, strength, love, expectation, understanding, knowledge, the word and most of all patience. Get your weapons out. Use them. You can make it. I can do all things through Christ that strengthens me.

Gratefulness. Know that He is always pulling out of you what is in you. There are different levels and the higher you go the more difficult the enemy will fight you, but God is greater, and He is with you. You are never alone. I won't leave nor forsake you. Ask the Lord what is it that you would have me to get from this.

When I was a babe in Christ, He gave me a weapon that helped me to face my greatest challenge to date. To know that against all odds my son would live, and not only did he live but he fought and taught me how to face fears, demons, how to see myself, how to see strengths as well as my weaknesses. God used him to pull out of me something

I never knew I had inside. And when his job was done, he went home to be with the Lord. The pain of losing him did not compare to the knowledge of the battles we fought and the understanding that his soul was at peace and rests in the arms of the Lord. Because truth be told, that was the answer to my initial prayer.

God doesn't waste anything. Everything is for a reason and for His purpose and plan. It ain't easy and many times as my son would say " You think this fun? This ain't fun mama." But it is worth the sacrifice. God says the suffering of today are not worthy to compare to the glory which shall be revealed to us. To God be the Glory! But I thank God for the opportunity to care for him at home in 2020. He was happy, I was excited, and we had a battle, but we won. And best of all he said to me "It was necessary. Everything was necessary." Prayers of the righteous availeth much.

It's About Process

As God is pouring out His spirit in this season, the time is now to get to know Him. I truly believe He has brought this time about to release us from mental bondage. Once we realize that we are free and that He is our source, nothing can hold us. We must learn to fight the enemy a different way. The Lord is teaching us how to fight spiritually.

We must spend more time in God's word. Spend time in prayer and learn to pray God's word. He told me to speak His language. He later told me to be ready to give a word to those He sends to me, and I am trying to do just that. I move in expectation of my next assignment from God. If He sends me someplace, I know that He will give me a word for someone in that place.

Be prepared to move in expectation that He will do just what He said. Wait for the manifestation of His promises. Look and expect great things. In this season we can confidently watch the word of God come alive, just as John 1:14 describes.

When Corion said, *"Let him do His thang ma"* the Holy Spirit revealed that it was about process. We must stay in the process, handle the fire, walk and not run. Though we become weary, we must not faint in our well doing. An impetuous spirit would have us to run rather than walk. Walking allows us to take in the view and therefore see the miracles unfolding.

Prayer will not change process, nor does God need our permission. We must trust the process, even when it is difficult. We do not know the outcome of the assignment. However, we gain clarity in hindsight if we remain connected to the Father for the updates on the plan.

Romans 8:18-21
"I consider that our present sufferings are not worth comparing with the glory that will be revealed in us. For the creation waits in eager expectation for the children of God to be revealed. For the creation was subjected to frustration, not by its own choice, but by the will of the one who subjected it, in hope that the creation itself will be liberated from its bondage to decay and brought into the freedom and glory of the children of God."

Chapter 30
Eating Cookies

"But solid food is for the mature, for those who have their powers of discernment trained by constant practice to distinguish good from evil." Hebrews 5:15

Anyone that cared for Corion, or spent any time around him after his injury, remembers what he asked for more than anything else. COOKIES! I do not know where this passion came from, because it really wasn't apart of him before. He liked sweets, and after his injury, his first request was for a snack. But there was something different about this cookie fetish.

07/03/2018 (social media post)
This addiction to cookies is driving me crazy . He is downright violent when we won't give him more more more. I don't know what else to do . Making me really rethink this vacation next weekend......

Whenever I would come into his room and ask, "What you doing?" He'd always reply, *"Eating Cookies"*, but he wouldn't be eating anything most times. We always assumed he just loved eating cookies, and he definitely ate a lot of them over six years. But, based on the many other things he would tell me, I began to believe there was another meaning behind the cookies.

He told me once when I was visiting with him in his room, *"You should eat more cookies."* So, I said to myself, maybe he wants me to relax and chill out. Another time he said, *"God don't like your cookies and M&Ms."* So now I was confused again. He also said these things, *"The cookies are too heavy"*, *"I'm scared of the cookies"*, and *"I know what's wrong with me, it's the cookies"*. During our quarantine time together in 2020, I said to him one day, "You are going to have to tell me what these cookies mean before you leave me." He just smiled and chuckled a bit.

Even though he would talk about the cookies as if they were bad for him, during my journaling, I heard in the spirit, cookies are *"sweet words"*. So being who I am, and the person God created me to be, I had to go deeper to figure this thing out. I love words and searching out the meaning behind them. I'm always up for a good mystery and fact-finding mission. I'm a problem resolution type of person. I know there must be a deeper meaning behind the "cookies". I wasn't going to be satisfied with this memoir without addressing it.

I've began this chapter not completely understanding, but I believe the Holy Spirit will reveal this mystery. My process is much like putting the pieces of a puzzle together. First, I start with what I know to be true. Cookies are an earthly pleasure, many times they are sweet, but not always good for you. As a matter of fact, eating too many can make you sick. Even Corion found that out once or twice. I also tried to think of things in my current life that may be called cookies, other than the actual cookie we eat. Maybe in the spirit cookies were a symbol for the word.

Cookies as a Metaphor

God will use what you already know, to teach you and guide you. I know that there are several references in the bible where Jesus and the prophets used relatable symbolism to convey the word of God to the audience. So, I began to think about other ways the word "cookies" may be used in life today.

I became interested in computers during my first year in college. I use one daily for my job. I often thought about how the computer uses the term "cookies" as a metaphor to describe how data is tracked for websites and information about the user's activity. This includes the pages viewed, the content listened to, ads clicked, settings and other actions performed on each particular platform.

I recently asked the Holy Spirit to reveal the mystery of the cookies to me, and the spirit directed me one morning to search the internet for "spiritual cookies". I did just that and found several pictures of actual cookies, but there was one article, just one, entitled "Spiritual Cookies" (*The Gospel Coalition (TGC). (2008, April 29). Spiritual Cookies [Blog post]. Retrieved from https://www.thegospelcoalition.org/blogs/erik-raymond/spiritual-cookies/*). I was floored. The article not only referenced the same term of "cookies" in the way I thought, but the scriptures also put me in mind of Corion.

The Holy Spirit leaped inside of me as I took in every word of this article. The writer refers to our thoughts as spiritual cookies. He presents many thought-provoking questions about what we would find if we opened the "cookies file" in our mind. How many times have we visited with the Lord or his word? How many times do we seek God in prayer? The first scripture referenced:

Colossians 3:1-4
"Since, then, you have been raised with Christ, set your hearts on things above, where Christ is, seated at the right hand of God. Set your minds on things above, not on earthly things. For you died, and your life is now hidden with Christ in God. When Christ, who is your life, appears, then you also will appear with him in glory."

In the text, the Apostle Paul instructs the church to take their minds off the world's ways and set their affections on heavenly things. Once we profess Christ, we should begin to seek to set our minds on heavenly things. If we do so, we will glory with Christ at his appearing. Life today, is clearly showing signs of the imminent return of our Lord and Savior, Jesus Christ.

If I break down the scripture, I can see, that Corion was raised up with Christ and he was in deep thought (*Eating Cookies*) whenever I would visit him. As time went on, he became less and less concerned with the earthly things. Most importantly verse 3 references how a person has "died" (past tense) and their life is hidden in Christ in God. This may reference a spiritual death for the reader, but it also can reference a natural death in my son's case.

It's Deep Ain't It

I've already concluded that Corion could see things that I could not see. His life was hidden with Christ, and he will appear again with him in glory. That may be really deep for some to understand. It was really too deep for me at one time too. But my faith in Christ has grown to a point where I truly understand that Corion was having conversations with the Lord (*sweet words*) and trying to translate them to me the best way he knew how.

There was even a time early on when I walked into his room as he was in a full conversation by himself. He was saying how good he has been to him and how grateful He was for that. I asked, "Who are you talking to?" He replied, "*God*", as if I should have recognized Him sitting there, in the empty chair, listening. I then wished I had not interrupted him.

In order to receive and accept things of the spirit, we must first be connected to the spirit. How do we connect, but to spend time in the word and presence of God? We must allow the Holy Spirit to translate and intercede on our behalf. We must then believe and trust the word of God that is translated by the Spirit.

The article also referenced 2 Corinthians 10. *"Eating Cookies"* could mean him being in deep thought and/or prayer. During these times, he was seeking to arrest his thoughts about the things that he could see that we could not see. I am certain he knew more than most, the consequences of his thoughts, and the benefit to affixing them on heavenly things, despite the constant struggle he had in doing so. And as a final reference to the article text:

"Time is ticking, you and I have less time to make much of Christ than we did yesterday. Let's arrest our thoughts and affix them upon that which is today and forever will be infinitely glorious."

Just as the Lord knows I would, I read the entire chapter. Verse 10, caught my attention, and made me think of him saying, *"The cookies are too heavy."*

2 Corinthians 10:10
"For they say, "His letters are weighty and strong, but his bodily presence is weak, and his speech of no account."

The information he was thinking upon was powerful (heavy/weighty), but his body was weak, and no one considered the things he said of any importance. His thoughts also could have brought about fear and uncertainty for him. Even I had to stop to listen and consider that maybe he was truly trying to tell me something of value.

Paul is specific about what earthly natures we must put to death and rid ourselves of as believers. He lists the things we must clothe ourselves in, such as compassion, kindness, and patience. He admonishes that we forgive as the Lord has forgiven us. Over all these things we must use love to bind all things together in perfect unity. In verses 18-22, he provides instructions for everyone in the household.

The Bread of Life

The cookies were a big thing. My spirit wasn't satisfied with only this. I asked the Holy Spirit for something simpler to reference for those that may not be as mature in Christ or raised in Christ. One morning the Holy Spirit placed the passage of scripture in my spirit that said, "Take, eat; this is my body (Matthew 26:26)". I know this scripture speaks of the last supper. But it also suggests communion. Most believers are familiar with communion.

The passage of scripture references the Last Supper where Jesus gave thanks, then broke the bread, and gave it to his disciples to eat as a symbol of his body. He instructs them to do this in remembrance of Him which we call communion. I've studied this verse and others that reference this moment.

I remember a post I made when Corion had vanilla wafers for the first time after his injury. Wafers and cookies are much like bread. I began to study the scriptures, commentary and sermons on Jesus as the Bread of Life. I studied writings about the last supper, communion, the feeding of the multitude, and the devil tempting Him to turn the stones into bread.

08/09/2015 (social media post)
Him: Those cookies are wonderful bruh!
Me: Not wonderful! That mean you want one more.
Him: ONE! Mane naw; at least FIVE!
KMSL.......some of you understand how this makes me laugh and cry at the same time.

After the publishing of the eBook version, a sister-in-Christ, Patricia Wilson, led me to this scripture that speaks to the sweetness of the "cookies"

Exodus 16:31-32

Now the house of Israel called its name manna. It was like coriander seed, white, and the taste of it was like wafers made with honey. Moses said, "This is what the Lord has commanded: 'Let an omer of it be kept throughout your generations, so that they may see the bread with which I fed you in the wilderness, when I brought you out of the land of Egypt.

It took me several weeks of praying, seeking and study to come to some revelations. One is, when speaking, my son used food names as symbolism for something much deeper. God is sharpening my spiritual discernment weapon through this study. To God be the Glory!

John 6:27
"Do not work for food that spoils, but for food that endures to eternal life, which the Son of Man will give you. For on him God the Father has placed his seal of approval."

There were two verses in this chapter of John that could speak to the difficulty and challenge with grasping this revelation. In verse 60, many disciples said, "This is a hard teaching. Who can accept it?". Then in verse 66, several of the followers decided to walk away from Jesus. Often, the cares of life will challenge our way of thinking and require renewing our minds. We must always consider the character of the Lord is one of sincere love, and not to do harm. And I surely can't give up now.

I knew there had to be a deeper hidden meaning behind the cookies. I listened to a message, "The Bread of Heaven" by Bishop Jakes, that revealed a different understanding in the symbolism of Jesus breaking the bread. It takes several steps to prepare bread which feeds you, strengthens you and sustains you. However, in the spiritual sense, the Lord will make us as bread to feed his people. To become bread, we must endure the chastening; this is the breaking. Corion was broken to become as bread for God's people. The breaking allows us to stand as a testimony that you can survive.

Upon reading John 6, I conclude that Corion's eating of the cookies could have been symbolic of communing with Jesus. I can recall a moment when I told him "All the cookies are gone." He said, *"You sure! Ain't no cookies nowhere?"* I said, "No, not for you." He said, *"Cookies are all I got left in the world bruh."* He was very sad about this.

Corion's desire for cookies is certainly a lasting memory for many (remembrance). The lesson we can take from his insistence and persistence with eating cookies, is that we must earnestly give thanks and commune with Christ often, as Christ gave his body as a living sacrifice for us all. The cookies are symbolic of eating the bread of life. Jesus and the word of God are the bread of life. The bread of life is the acceptance in faith. This acceptance brings salvation and salvation brings eternal life.

It could be said that God had sustained him in the wilderness with His "manna" (cookies). But during the week, before he passed away, remember Corion woke up, looked to his father and asked for cornbread.

Matthew 7:9
"Or what man is there among you who, if his son asks for bread, will give him a stone?"

My friend Nancy and I was talking recently about my revelations. She said to me, "Much like children, God gives us cookies first to bring us in and then we get the cornbread which is the sustenance." God wants to feed us, but we must first learn to accept and believe on His son, who came to save us from sin that we may have eternal life.

Reading of this passage of scripture in Matthew 7, brings us to the understanding that *Corion* had been asking, seeking and knocking and our Heavenly Father promises to not withhold any good things from those that ask. My son's search was for eternal life. I believe this wholeheartedly because we discussed it often. He even said, *"Please call me a child of God."*

I've earnestly asked for answers in search of this revelation regarding the cookies, to share with all. As Corion said, *"Ask God for what you want."* **To God be the Glory!!**

John 6:37-40
"All those the Father gives me will come to me, and whoever comes to me I will never drive away. For I have come down from heaven not to do my will but to do the will of him who sent me. And this is the will of him who sent me, that I shall lose none of all those he has given me, but raise them up at the last day. For my Father's will is that everyone who looks to the Son and believes in him shall have eternal life, and I will raise them up at the last day."

What are you eating?

This chapter is truly longer than I desired, but I would be remiss not to discuss what we eat physically and what we eat spiritually. We must be discerning in what we feed ourselves physically as our health is our true wealth. No matter how much money you have, many times our health can be fleeting. Since writing this book I found this scripture about the importance of fasting that may be of great value to many, especially me.

Isaiah 58:8
"Then shall thy light break forth as the morning, and thine health shall spring forth speedily: and thy righteousness shall go before thee; the glory of the LORD shall be thy reward."

Fasting may not answer all our health issues, but I truly believe if the Lord said it, it has to be extremely important. My son said to me once,

"You too big." My feelings were truly hurt. But I began to lose weight. I need to do this again. Also, during his week of transition he said, *"The fat on them is bad on them."* I'm sure that this has a spiritual meaning as well which I will seek God for. But for now, I will take it literally and manage my diet, particularly incorporating fasting.

Fasting in the way described in Isaiah, can not only bring health and weight loss benefits, but it benefits me spiritually. I've become accustomed to fasting through the teachings of my Pastor, Sylvester Hamilton. He was adamant about this practice and truly a great man of God. My commitment to myself and the spirit is to work to improve my physical and spiritual diet daily. I do this in honor of both my son and my mother, who passed away with health issues.

Just as we must be careful of the things we consume through eating. We must also be just as careful with the things we consume as information. I studied many scriptures and was able to seek God and other trusted resources He has pressed upon me for information. We must seek the Holy Spirit for discernment in the words, music and voices we consume spiritually.

We can't just satisfy the flesh. The scripture tells us man can't live on bread alone but by every word from God. It's difficult to grasp and some may walk away. But if we only feed the flesh, we will be unable to control ourselves and not be satisfied. We must feed on God's word which is the bread of life. Corion asked for cornbread in the end. He wanted something of more sustenance. He was searching for eternal life. He said he asked, and God provided.

Jesus is the bread of life in the word of God. We receive Him in faith. He is the only way to everlasting life.

1 John 5:11
"Truly, truly, I say to you, he who hears My word, and believes Him who sent Me, has eternal life, and does not come into judgment, but has passed out of death into life."

The entire chapter of John 6 served as a great resource in my discerning this subject about the cookies. Here's another revelation. Corion said to me one day while I was feeding him, *"Yall got fake food here to huh?"* I was shocked. Wow. What does that mean? Was this salmon he was eating fake? I'm not sure, but I know he didn't like it. But in my study of this chapter, I happened upon a word from God.

John 6:55
"For my flesh is real food and my blood is real drink."

With my current spiritual knowledge, I understand we must seek natural solutions in this world, but more importantly, spiritual understanding. Truth regarding life can always be found in the word of God. The word assures us the world will not understand things of the spirit. Thinking on and consuming Godly things limits the amount of control the enemy can wage against us.

I've learned that changing our words, thoughts, and perspectives, will change our life. My goal is to meditate on heavenly things, as I believe Corion did, when he would reply that he was *"eating cookies"*. Changing the atmosphere is important. Also, I believe feeding the mind and body the right things will help conform thoughts, mind and body in righteousness.

Romans 12:1-2
"Therefore, I urge you, brothers and sisters, in view of God's mercy, to offer your bodies as a living sacrifice, holy and pleasing to God—this is your true and proper worship. Do not conform to the pattern of this world, but be transformed by the renewing of your mind. Then you will be able to test and approve what God's will is—his good, pleasing and perfect will."

Chapter 31
Not Seen and Yet Believed

"Jesus said to him, 'Have you believed because you have seen me? Blessed are those who have not seen and yet have believed.'" John 20:29

Corion's life and our journey is my evidence that God is real. It was through him I realized that God was speaking to me. I was told by a prophet and two sisters-in-law, that the enemy was really after me, not Corion. Maybe I just didn't want to accept it. But once he transitioned, an anointing fell upon me that I couldn't deny.

Many questioned my peace, and some waited patiently for me to fall apart. Yes, I've cried and grieved the loss of my beloved son. I've questioned why things went the way they have gone. I feel the pain and loss. But the knowledge of God and His ever-present spirit gives me a comfort that surpasses all understanding. The anointing makes us free, even when everything around us is in chains.

To give you an example, the pain of childbirth in the throes of labor can feel unbearable. But once you see your child, the gift seems worth the pain. The pain of the past six years and the ultimate passing of my son was a pain that frequently felt unbearable. But it was worth the pain, knowing that his soul rests in the Lord.

When I was a babe in Christ, God gave me the scripture, "lean not to thine own understanding" regarding a situation. When I think back, He has armed me with many scriptures by allowing me to be my Pastor's reader during church services. He's led me and guided me to this very hour. He showed me His supernatural spirit through my son's life in many ways.

I know for sure that I must share our experience with anyone that God places in my path. It's not something I would have done so boldly before this time, especially not with strangers. But it seems I have no fear in telling others about the love of God and His presence right now. He breathed His breath in each one of us. He is inside of you. It's the gift of life. He wants you to acknowledge Him, become aware of His presence and allow Him to lead and guide you through your obedience to His word and instruction.

1 Thessalonians 4:13-14
"Brothers and sisters, we do not want you to be uninformed about those who sleep in death, so that you do not grieve like the rest of mankind, who have no hope. For we believe that Jesus died and rose again, and so we believe that God will bring with Jesus those who have fallen asleep in him."

The Evidence

I am convinced, God used Corion to be a vessel! He is our evidence that God is Real. According to man, he should have been dead or a vegetable. I recall one nurse said he didn't look like what his chart said. She surely didn't expect to see a man having full conversations. She especially didn't anticipate that he would be so strong. But GOD! His grace is sufficient.

My evidence is the answered prayers. The secret conversations between me and God, or even the questions between Corion and I, have been answered through my interactions with others, in sermons, songs and especially through scripture. God is knocking at the door of many hearts, especially the young. If you want to see the evidence, have a secret sincere conversation with God. Take some time to sit still and quiet listening for the voice of the spirit.

Then later, when you are not looking for it, an answer to your prayer WILL COME. It may not always feel good nor be the answer you were hoping for, but it will be an answer just the same. The evidence, I mean the answer, may come in the form of a word from someone, an act of kindness, or even something small that resonates with that secret conversation. Try it. It is what has kept me through the most difficult uncertain time of my life.

More evidence is in my plea for Corion's life in the ER. I stated that I truly believe that he could be a testimony to God's kingdom. Well, every time I have an opportunity, I tell someone about my son and our journey. Even more telling, I recently learned that Corion told Jasmine (Jacori's mom) that he knew God had a purpose for him. She remembers him specifically stating long before his illnesses, *"I think I'm supposed to be a prophet or something."* He is truly a testimony to God's kingdom and the evidence of things not seen.

Psalm 106:8
"Yet he saved them for his name's sake, to make his mighty power known."

Things Not Seen

Our bodies are earthly vessels. They serve as a container for the Holy Spirit. The body must be seen (visible) for man to experience a move of God. It's often said we are the hands and feet of God. Many times, we must see it to believe it. But the real treasures are things that cannot be seen.

Our story had an impact on people I've never met or known across the internet. Others had a chance to share in our miracles, without having known us personally, nor be there to see it with their own eyes. My good friend, Iris, told me of her friend who followed our story on social media and its impact on her. To this day I haven't had the pleasure of meeting her, however, the glory belongs to God. He will use our circumstances and trials to help others without our knowledge.

The impact of God's word through the many messengers I've referenced in this book also amazes me. I've never met the Pastors I've followed on the internet this year, and they surely know nothing of our journey, but their ministry seems to speak directly to me and our circumstances. We may never see the effect of the work we do as messengers for the Lord, but it does not diminish the value of its presence in the earth.

God uses the Holy Spirit to bring things forth through scripture. It's not like it isn't always there. But as you seek for understanding, He lifts the veil so that we can see in the natural what is visible in the spiritual realm. We must take the time to focus not so much on the things that we can see, but begin to reverence, acknowledge, and be thankful for the things we cannot see, feel and touch. The world is based on the things you can see, while the spiritual realm cannot be seen but is very real. We can no longer see, touch or feel Corion, but God left us his spirit as a gift of his love. For that, we are truly thankful.

True Faith

I can now understand that God's plan from the beginning was much greater than I could ask or think. Not only to give me an anointing for the assignment He has on my life, but also to heal me from the many issues within my heart. We must exercise our faith. You will not realize God is all you need until God is all you've got.

The truth about your faith journey will show when you don't get your way and must succumb to God's way. God showed me myself when things don't go the way I think they should go. It wasn't a pretty picture, I must admit. To say you trust God is one thing, but the real work begins when God is all you have. Having to believe when others don't believe, forces you to move forward, clinging to expectation and hope. It gets lonely, but your relationship with God becomes so much stronger.

Dear God, please help me remember that true faith is not receiving what I want from You. It is graciously accepting what You give me.

Matthew 26:41
"Watch and pray, that ye enter not into temptation: the spirit indeed is willing, but the flesh is weak."

Crazy Faith

God will use the pressure of life to bring you into freedom. It's intended to grow your faith. Crooked paths are made straight. The more you trust God, the more you exercise and build that faith muscle.

Many believers have read or heard a sermon preached about Peter's miraculous escape from prison chronicled in Acts 12:1-18. Peter walked out of prison escorted by an angel. But as I am led by the Holy Spirit and my new love for God's word, I can now see more details in these passages that hadn't been pointed out to me before. God doesn't waste anything in our lives, especially words. Words are very important.

The writer sets the scene as to why Peter was in prison and, more importantly, how many soldiers were guarding him, four squads of four soldiers each. That would be sixteen (16) soldiers guarding this one man. No matter how many odds are against you, God only needs one (1) angel, one plan for His will to be done. I could stop right there but keep reading.

The scripture makes sure to tell the reader in verse 5 that the church was earnestly praying to God for him. Earnestly praying suggests that they were pleading with God on his behalf that he would not meet the same fate as James and John, who had been put to death with the sword. It's no doubt the church members were asking God to spare Peter's life. They didn't know how, but as they were taught, they prayed hoping that He would answer.

In verse 6, the writer describes how Peter had a trial soon, but what was he doing? He was sleeping between two soldiers! This mane was comfortable! How are you sleep, bound with two chains between two soldiers, with at least 14 soldiers keeping guard at the entrance, and a trial just a few hours away, where he would be surely put to death in a public setting? I can already tell you I wouldn't have been asleep. I have stayed up many nights worried about far less than being put to death. Lord help me!

However, that was the plan of the enemy. But God! Suddenly, cause God does things suddenly, an angel woke him up and told him to get up quick, and the chains fell off his wrists. But what I find even more interesting is that he had to tell Peter to get dressed. You have some crazy faith to take your shoes off and get undressed under these circumstances.

Peter got up, put on his clothes, sandals, and wrapped himself in his cloak as the angel instructed. Verse 9 tells you that he followed the angel out of prison, but he had no idea it was real; he thought he was having a vision. God will blow your mind. If you follow the leading of the Holy Spirit, trusting that God will provide according to His riches and glory, He will do the things that you cannot do in your own might.

The angel led Peter past the guards, through the gate which opened by itself. God will open doors that don't require your touch. You don't have to place your hand on it. Your job is to allow your faith, trust, belief, and obedience to drive. Life isn't all about what we can do for ourselves, but more about allowing God to work within you so that His purpose and plans for our lives may be fulfilled.

Peter walked the length of the street and again suddenly, the angel left, just as quickly as he had come. The Holy Spirit will walk with you, lead, guide and protect you. One of the gates opened by itself. There will be some doors that open with no effort on your part. That's when we truly know God is in the midst. The angel leaving him, confirms there will be moments when you must walk alone in your faith.

Verse 11 tells us Peter came to himself and said, "Now I have no doubt..." Because of the miracles I've seen and experienced with Corion, I have no doubt of the goodness, glory, mercy, grace, protection, strength, and love of God. He has shown Himself faithful to His word and His promises in our life.

Peter went to the house of Mary where they were gathered in earnest prayer. Rhoda answered the door and was excited by his voice. But strangely enough, the ***earnestly praying*** church folk told her she was delusional. Now why were they earnestly praying but not expecting the answer they were praying for? We must pray in a posture of expectancy. We must believe for what we are praying for. Or maybe they had their minds set on what the answer would look like. I was crazy enough to believe that God would allow Corion to be fully healed and I still believe he would have. It just wasn't Corion's desire.

Where are your expectations when you are praying? We must not only pray, but pray with the confidence and expectation of manifestation, regardless of the circumstances or what it looks like. And when you don't know what to say, the perfect prayer is, "God's will be done." It may look like you are losing, but God will step in and finish the fight for you. The answer may not look as we desire, but if I believe for God's will, I accept His will is perfect. When He places His hands on it, it is well.

I am ecstatic as to how this verse speaks to me in a way, far different than it has in the past. My favorite part of the scripture is the latter part of verse 11 that reveals Peter was not only rescued from Herod's clutches, but from the expectation of the others looking forward to his demise. Isn't it awesome to know that the expectations of the enemy does not determine your outcome!

Chapter 32

God is in the Questions

"My brothers, if anyone among you wanders from the truth and someone brings him back, let him know that whoever brings back a sinner from his wandering will save his soul from death and will cover a multitude of sins." James 5:19-20

Just like an escape room, the answers and clues you find in one "room" in this life, will lead you to more questions and more answers, that lead to yet another "room," and then another, until you have found your way of escape.

Believing that we can manage life and this world without the knowledge of God is truly a facade. The word says, "For God so loved the world that he gave His only begotten son. For whosoever believeth in Him shall not perish but have everlasting life" (John 3:16).

We fear death, but death is merely the next level of life. Corion was willing to face death in exchange for everlasting life. I am so proud of him. He always told me, *"I know more than you know."* At first, I didn't really listen, nor try to understand. He once said, *"Do you believe me ma, do you believe me? I just want you to believe me."* I wanted to believe him; I just couldn't understand what any of it meant. As I began to ask, seek and pray, the Lord opened up my understanding.

Christ overcame death. He conquered death. Our knowledge of God should help us to conquer the fear of death. Overcoming the fear of death, activates our ability to live free.

I can now confidently proclaim to Corion, "I believe you baby. I truly believe you and I love you so much for waiting until I was ready to accept who you were, so that I can become aware of who I am and who God is." Corion was operating from another realm, somewhere between life and death. In the spiritual realm nothing is hidden. In my acceptance of Corion's truth, I can fully accept the truth of God's word. Because of this I am a witness of His mercy and grace. We all are.

This book, the representation of Corion's request to *"write everything down, we gone change the world"*, may just as well be the reference he made to *"this going all over the country; all over the nation."* Our prayers may not have been answered in the way we wanted, nor look the way we imagined, but no doubt Corion serves as a testimony to God's kingdom. I found where he wrote one of his dream jobs was to be a preacher. For me, he accomplished that!

2020 Revelation

It wasn't until after my son took his last breath on September 05, 2020, that God began to reveal to me what it all meant. During a quiet moment the day after his passing, the Holy Spirit spoke to me, "Remember your prayer?", referring to my plea in the ER. I did remember. I was praying for Corion to not die without time to get his life right with the Lord.

I did not want his soul to go to hell. God clearly said to me, "The fight was never about his body. That was the distraction. The fight was always about his soul. The enemy disguised himself as a brain injury." That was huge for me. It was about his SOUL!

We were fighting for his soul to rest in Heaven. That's why Corion told me the week of his transition, *"You Won!"* He had said to me in 2014, *"No one knew what to do, but you did. I love you for that."* I always considered he was referring to my praying in the ER on that day of his first death. I can also remember him saying once, *"I'm so glad you my momma. I'm so proud of you ma."* I will always treasure these words.

So, as many may be discouraged, or better said, distracted by the fact that he didn't get up and walk, or go back to the life he lived before, I am assured that this was never the plan. Corion's healing was about the healing of his soul. He was to a point where he was able to make the decision to not continue trying to preserve his earthly body. He knew he had *"another house waiting for him"*. He was prepared to exchange this earthly life for everlasting life in the Kingdom of Heaven.

It can be difficult to accept for some, but I had to respect his wishes as the mother of an adult man. I was happy that he had the ability to make his own decision with such understanding and decisiveness, which was a miracle. As a believer, I can recognize that God's plans are much greater than our plans. I much rather his fate be about his eternal life, than this temporary life on earth.

The Holy Spirit let me know, God used my son to help me because He knew I would not believe anyone else. Because of my childhood and past, I have many trust issues. That's why I know my husband loves me, because that poor man must be the most patient man on this earth to deal with my craziness sometimes. LOL

Love Is

As a little girl, I can remember my aunt Rochelle used to have these little cartoons that said, "Love Is". One in particular read, "Love is…..what helps you take everything life throws at you." It is difficult to define love, as it is different for each individual. Love for some may be a feeling while for others it is more of an obligation.

For me love had always been on condition. If you loved me or showed me love, then I could reciprocate it. However, this journey has grown my understanding of love. It's not just a warm feeling, but also something tangible and necessary. I've learned to love beyond the boundaries of reciprocity to a level of unconditional love.

God's love and knowing that He loves me beyond my flaws, has taught me what love is for me. If He can love me in spite of my sin, I can strive to show that same love to others. We all need someone at some point. I believe for most people, 2020 proved that to be true. I'm convinced, until you fall in love with Jesus and build a relationship with Him, you won't know true love.

I admonish everyone to build a relationship with Him. A relationship requires time and intimacy. Quiet moments together, consistent communication, trust, and love. I feel qualified in saying this, because I've been married to the same man since I was a young lady. It has taken intimacy for us to build trust and continue to maintain a loving relationship. Intimacy equates to vulnerability. That's the relationship I now have with the Lord. His love for me will never change. Knowing this gives me a new definition of love; one that lines up with His word.

1 Corinthians 13:4-7
"Love is patient, love is kind. It does not envy, it does not boast, it is not proud. It does not dishonor others, it is not self-seeking, it is not easily angered, it keeps no record of wrongs. Love does not delight in evil but rejoices with the truth. It always protects, always trusts, always hopes, always perseveres."

The Anointing Breaks the Yoke

The "strength" that many used to describe me, when they say, "you are so strong", was not of my own, but by God's anointing. The scripture tells us that the anointing breaks the yoke. The yoke is something that binds you or holds you back. God had anointed me for this journey. I didn't know it at the time; nor did I understand it. The anointing helped me to keep moving forward despite the circumstances. A recent Jakes sermon (Anointed Alignment) said it like this, "The anointing comes to work! When God sends an anointing, He is enabling you to do what you could not do in your own strength."

I've always known that the joy that I have is from God. I felt pain, brokenness, and uncertainty, but the joy of the Lord is my strength. Whenever I would be confronted with doubt and fear, He would send a word, a friend, or a stranger to encourage me and remind me that He was in control. I was glad because this thing was hard. I needed and wanted someone else to help me carry the load.

Acknowledging God's presence was easier than trying to live life ignoring Him. People have often asked and wondered how I am able to continue to have joy during such adversity. As my awareness and acknowledgment of His presence grows, so does the anointing. It isn't in my own ability as a human, but it is by His power and might. It's the indwelling spirit of God within me in the form of the Holy Spirit that Christ left on record to be our comforter.

Everyone Has a Story

Many times, we could be watching the same movie but having two completely different experiences. When my sister and I tell a story about a childhood experience, she may have taken it one way, and I took it completely differently. However, no matter our different experiences, if we could respect the other person's experience and viewpoint, I believe we could possibly co-exist peacefully.

We all have a story. We all have a testimony. Don't be afraid to tell your testimony when you see the opportunity. Your kindness creates opportunity for your witness. Always remember that you carry God with you and that the comforter, His Holy Spirit, stands alongside to help. Trust God to give you the words, as we would fail in our own strength. Stand by and watch God work through you.

Let's pray for one another. Let's grow in our love for one another. Let's be patient with each other. Let's change this world together. God is raising up an army. By sharing our stories, we can then complete the work we are purposed for in this earth and live eternal life with the Father in heaven. That is my life-long endeavor. I too would love to see that beautiful place my son saw when he ran upstairs. Find your circle and link up. Make connections. We can grow together, rebuild, and watch God work. One young lady I spoke had the pleasure to witness to in a phone conversation said it this way, "We can make God *'touchable'* for others." I love that!

God is Concerned

After Corion's departure, I began to think differently about all the questions he asked over the years. Do you believe me? Do you see me? Do you know me? Do you love me? Where your love at? You still having fun? You still love me? Who are you? We must know God's language to understand that He speaks in questions. In my notes from a sermon, I found that it's not in the answers but in the questions, where you find out that God is Real and that there is a kingdom within you. The Lord is in the questions.

If I think about these questions in terms of the Lord, I can then see the true meaning of this journey. God is asking the exact same questions to His people, in terms of our relationship with Him. In our pursuit, God gave Corion and me a second chance. Everyone doesn't get the opportunity to try and right some wrongs. His chance was about eternal life and mines was about living a better life on earth. God wants everyone to be saved. He is now able to use me as a vessel for His purpose.

As we go through tough seasons in our lives, we often give up because we don't get the answers we want. But maybe we are not asking God the right questions. His word tells us to ask, seek and knock. That progression in that scripture speaks to the fact that there are levels. We want Him to just change our circumstances, but we must go deeper and confront the pain. I wanted to avoid the painful places but staying on that level only got me so far. In avoiding the pain, I did not feel a sense of relief.

My questions got past surface as the pain in my heart increased. I had turned my face to God every day to seek answers. I had learned to ask the questions that confronted the painful places. I asked, why does this affect me this way? Why does this hurt me so bad? What is it behind this emotional pain? When was the first time I felt this level of hurt/pain? What does this say about me? When things affect us deeply and passionately it is more about us than those that cause the pain. We must look deeper within and ask the Lord to reveal the source of the pain. It is normally tied to a memory that your spirit has not forgotten.

You have to go deep to find the source. Once you find the root and speak it out, healing begins. When the pain is exposed to the light, it can no longer control you or distract you from where God is taking you. Identifying the pain, finding the root and speaking it out is how we turn the light on the enemy. The light is Christ, who is the bread of life. This is how we began to grow in a deeper relationship with the Father. For we wrestle not against flesh and blood but powers in dark places.

1 Peter 2:9
"But you are a chosen people, a royal priesthood, a holy nation, God's special possession, that you may declare the praises of him who called you out of darkness into his wonderful light."

God Provides

God's word confirms that everything we need for this life is already inside. You have access thru the Holy Spirit. We try so hard to add to ourselves. We spend most of our lives using external means to bring joy and happiness to ourselves. But God's way is the law of subtraction. His way requires fewer external things and more spiritual things.

I know I always want to make sure I have everything I need when I take a trip. I try to prepare for every possible occasion. Then end up hauling all those unworn shoes and clothing back to the house, only to sit in the suitcase for weeks before I have the energy to unpack. Yeah, I said it!

The Lord told Gideon he had too many soldiers. He told the disciples to take nothing for their journey except a staff. He will provide what is needed along the way. I felt inadequate and unequipped for the journey with Corion because I didn't know the end. God provided all the people and knowledge needed along the way.

Mark 6:7-9
"He charged them to take nothing for their journey except a staff-no bread, no bag, no money in their belts – but to wear sandals and not put on two tunics."

This journey could have bankrupted us. There were many expenses we had to pay for ourselves. We were fortunate enough not to have to ask anyone for anything financially. That is evidence of the divine presence of the most high. Although there were times when I wasn't sure where the money would come from, I was able to pay a sitter to sit with Corion for six years. He had everything he needed, anytime he needed it. All our needs have been met. God always provided and continues to give us the health, strength, and means to manage our family well. God can be trusted to provide. It builds our faith and reliance on the Father. We must remain connected to Him for step-by-step instructions because we don't know the conclusion. We must remember the glory belongs to Him.

Philippians 4:19
"And my God will meet all your needs according to the riches of his glory in Christ Jesus."

To God be the Glory

While we go through the seasons, we can't get to the good part until we make it through the hard part. Try to think of adversity as your opportunity to have an experience with God that will sometimes provide a platform for you to stand and proclaim His glory. He will orchestrate moments so that someone else's miracle is connected to you. He is strategic like that. He is so AMAZING! It's not because we deserve it but to bring glory to His name and the kingdom.

I was motivated to keep going by the promise from God that this was bigger than me and bigger than Corion. I waited and moved in a posture of expectancy. God brought us this way for His name's sake. I pray that our journey provides comfort and strength to someone else's path on this earth.

Corion tried to tell me so many things, and I wanted to share as many as I can remember and understand with you. His relationship with God allowed him to share something that I could not see, but I knew they

216

were there through him. Now my task is to relay things that I can see to others, to help them see a way through their journey.

He embodied all the things I hoped for in faith. I sincerely pray that Corion's life and our journey may serve as evidence for a future generation to know the Lord and prove to them that He can be trusted.

"God is real. He has everything laid out. You don't even have to wonder."

2 Corinthians 4:17-18
"For our present troubles are small and won't last very long. Yet they produce for us a glory that vastly outweighs them and will last forever. So we don't look at the troubles we can see now; rather, we fix our gaze on things that cannot be seen. For the things we see now will soon be gone, but the things we cannot see will last forever."

To God be the Glory!!
AMEN

CORION D'SHAWN REED

25th Wedding Anniversary Party – September 2018
Grand Entrance escorted by Crystal Reed

Acknowledgments...

In this journey, God blessed us with so many angels along the way. I believe that this is part of the "circles," other than our family and close friends, that Corion spoke of in his last days with me.

In no particular order, Thank You!

Elder & Mrs. Sylvester Hamilton, Miracle Temple COGIC

Minister Willie & Janie Mae Dodson

Paragon Bank Work Family

Dr. Davis, Dr. Grant & Staff of Interventional Nephrology

Dr. Nezagatgoo

Dr. Christopher Green & Dr. Rayder

Dr. Stephnakowski & Dr. Ruiz

Fresenius Mt. Moriah Dialysis Center Staff

Allenbrooke Nursing & Rehabilitation – West Hall Staff

Health Care Transport (HCT)

Methodist University Hospital

Nurses – Stacy B., Timarako, John, Erica and Sandra

CNAs – Mrs. Sandra, Allisa, Candace, Daphne, Bobby & countless others

Long Term Sitters - Patricia B. & Candace H.

Barbers – Sherry and Lynn Stewart, Willie Dodson & His Pop

His Most Loyal Friends - Arbeny, Jason, Derrick, & Jasmine L.

Cookie Fairy - Tiffany Phillips (Cousin); Donna Baines (Co-worker) & Nancy Walls (Friend)

His Affirmations...

If God is for us, who can be against us? Roman 8:31

If God raised you from your death bed, He can remove this evil spirit and use you for His glory.

He has brought you from sickness after sickness after sickness.

He's healed you from infection, after infection, after infection, after infection

He's healed you from catheter after catheter, after catheter, after catheter, after catheter, to a point I lost count

He's moved your dialysis access from your left arm to your neck, to your chest, to your right arm and now your groin, which you weren't supposed to leave the hospital with almost 2 years ago.

He's taken you from not breathing, to breathing on a machine, to breathing through a trach in your neck, to breathing on your own.

He's taken you from closed mouth, to muffled speech, to mumbled language, to repeating what the tv says, to speaking in short phrases, to speaking in sentences, to now cursing like you don't have a global anoxic brain injury

He's taken you from not moving nor responding, to barely squeezing our hands, to moving your right leg, to reaching to scratch your nose with your left hand, to trying to hold my necklace, to holding the toothbrush, to holding the remote, to holding a cup, to holding a spoon, to catching a ball and throwing a ball, to swinging and trying to fight me

He's taken you from closed eyes, to opening your eyes, to tracking movement, to blinking your eyes, to saying you can't see, to watching tv, to playing the video game, to laughing at what you see on the television

He took you from no understanding, and no memory, to remembering your name, to remembering your birthday, to remembering names, to remembering dates, to remembering moments, remembering your address and phone number, to remembering the words of songs and singing them clearly, and saying the prayer before we eat and the ability to follow commands

He's taken you from feeding tube, to eating ice, to eating pureed food, to eating solid food, to being spoon fed, to feeding yourself

He took you from sleepless days and nights to full nights of sleep

He took you from grinding your teeth all day and night, to wearing a mouth guard, to only doing it on occasion

So, you cannot tell me what GOD CAN'T DO because He has ALREADY done more than we could ask or think

God says HE WILL BE WITH YOU! Trust HIM!

His Obituary...

Corion D'Shawn Reed was born December 25, 1987, to Leland Watson and Chondrea Reed in Memphis, TN. When Corion was three years old, his mother met and later married Robert Black who he affectionately referred to as "Pop." They attended Miracle Temple Church of God in Christ in Victoria, MS, where he would profess Christ at an early age under the leadership of Elder Sylvester Hamilton.

Corion was always a fun-loving, caring, and charismatic young man. He enjoyed basketball, building friendships, and making others laugh. He attended Kirby, Ridgeway, and later Overton High School where he graduated in 2006. While attending Southwest Community College he celebrated the birth of his son Jacori Reed, with Jasmine Dodson (Derrick). During his tenure at Arkansas State University in Jonesboro, AR, he began experiencing health challenges, and Jacori became his reason to live.

His health battles were always met with strength in character and a strong will to fight, as he had always possessed. He never wanted anyone to feel sorry for him or even know he was ill. He was able to channel this energy towards his will to live, not as much for himself, but for those that loved and needed him.

In 2014, Corion met his greatest challenge which resulted in total disability, however his resilience, genuine faith, and capacity for love once again helped him beat all odds stacked against him. Though his prognosis was grim, his will was strong, and he continued to live, laugh, love, bring joy and strive to enjoy life despite his condition. One of the most admirable traits was his smile, which they predicted would not be possible for him after his injury, BUT GOD!

After six years, many surgeries and near-death illness, Mr. Reed, made the brave decision himself to place his life completely in the Master's hands and look death in the eye, in exchange for everlasting life. With a personal relationship with God, profession of Christ for salvation and a clean heart, he peacefully departed this life on Saturday September 5, 2020. He was surrounded by his parents and son, as he transitioned "upstairs to a beautiful place" where he was rejoined to his beloved grandmother, Jackie Reed who preceded him in death.

Though his time on this earth was not long, Corion wasted no time touching many lives during his 32 years. He always left an indelible impact on anyone who crossed his path through his personal pursuit to put a smile on their face and joy in their hearts despite his own daily challenges. Many would agree that he managed to excel at this very task.

Corion leaves to celebrate his life, his son, Jacori, his parents Robert and Chondrea Black, his father Leland Watson along with his grandmother, Gloria Watson, and their family; his baby sister Danielle Black and his adored nephew and niece, Jace and Aria; his cherished aunts Ericka Hayes and Crystal Reed; his grandfather Reginald Green, great grandfather Willie Green (Dorothy), great grandmother Martha Harris (Joe), two aunts, an uncle, their spouses and first cousins. Corion was joined into the Black family by marriage but bound by love. He leaves four loving uncles Larry Humphrey, Anthony Humphrey, Andre Black (Lakitta), Christopher Black; four supportive aunts, Lisa Milan (Jasper), Laura Isom, Shawnece Harris, and Sharon Black. He leaves a host of great aunts, uncles, cousins, church family, and friends. (09/13/20)

ABOUT THE AUTHOR

"God is Real…You don't even have to wonder" is the first published work by author, **Chondrea Black**. She attributes her passion for writing to

her mother, Jacquelyne Reed. Black has served as contributing writer for several published projects for others and produced storybooks for her family. She has enjoyed a lengthy career in banking and currently works as First Vice President of Credit and Compliance for Paragon Bank. She credits her maternal grandmother, Corrine Reed Wall, for her strong spiritual foundation. After her union to, husband, Robert Black in 1993, she joined his family church, Miracle Temple COGIC, under the leadership of Elder Sylvester Hamilton. Here, where they also raised their children in holiness, she gained a greater understanding of scripture, salvation, righteousness and the gift of the Holy Spirit. She is a committed servant of God and woman of great faith.

1 Corinthians 2:1-5
And I, brethren, when I came to you, came not with excellency of speech or of wisdom, declaring unto you the testimony of God. For I determined not to know anything among you, save Jesus Christ, and him crucified. And I was with you in weakness, and in fear, and in much trembling. And my speech and my preaching was not with enticing words of man's wisdom, but in demonstration of the Spirit and of power: That your faith should not stand in the wisdom of men, but in the power of God.

WELCOME TO THE CIRCLE!

Want to join the discussion? Meet me on Facebook in our private group, *The Circle*

To request Chondrea Black for speaking engagements, podcasts, or inquire about bulk book purchases and more, visit our website at www.corionsmom.com

For more from this author, sign-up on the website to receive emailed blog posts. Also we ask that you please take a moment to leave an honest review on Amazon. Thanks in advance.

See you in the Circle

FOLLOW US

Facebook/Chondrea.Black
Instagram @corionsmom
www.corionsmom.com

hashtags: #GodisReal #watchGodwork #prayerworks #RILCorion #TGBTG

Made in the USA
Columbia, SC
25 November 2023

27099415R00130